The Stuart Little Band

A Mouse That Almost Roared

David Holem

This is, to the best of my recollection, a true story of some young musicians from the Central Valley of California seeking fame and fortune in the music industry during the tumultuous late 1960's and early 1970's. I have pieced together this story from conversations with Stephen Solari and Scott Liggett, referencing various websites and a collection of letters that I wrote to my girlfriend and wife-to-be, Debra. I apologize for any errors and omissions that I can only attribute to my faulty memory of events that transpired forty or more years ago.

The war in Vietnam had reached its peak during this period. The last man drafted was on June 30, 1973. The war ended 21 months later when Saigon fell to the North Vietnamese Army on April 30, 1975. We knew many who served in the armed forces during this time, some of whom were among the 58,220 who lost their lives in the conflict. I wish to extend my gratitude to all those who sacrificed and my condolences to those families who lost a loved one.

Table of Contents

Preface: A Quest for Fame and Fortune

Follow the way of music, Ravel...
Follow the way of music

—*The Dream, Gordon Clark*

In the early1970's live music was everywhere and everybody knew someone who played in a band. Of course, there were the big, established acts that drew huge crowds and had lots of airplay and album sales. These included The Beatles, Rolling Stones, Jefferson Airplane, Grateful Dead, Simon and Garfunkel, the Guess Who, Jackson 5, Three Dog Night, the Temptations, Rod Stewart, Elton John, Eagles, Zombies, the Doors, Sly and the Family Stone, The Who, Credence Clearwater Revival, Chicago, Joe Cocker, Santana, Led Zeppelin, and many, many more.

In addition to those bands that everyone knew, there were tens of thousands of garage bands where a bunch of friends got together and started hammering out their cover versions of the big hits. They played in the local bars, down at the park, friend's parties, and occasional weddings. These guys (and it was mostly guys) were just having a good time, picking up a little extra cash, and gaining notoriety with their friends.

There was another tier of musicians that probably started in a garage somewhere, but somehow became infected with the "I want to make it big" bug. These guys wrote their own material, rehearsed extra hard, and kept pushing for more attention and a bigger audience, hoping to attract the notice of a big Hollywood producer or record company. Bands that were this dedicated developed their own sound and style and became well known in their local environment. They traveled as much as possible for maximum exposure and experience. What little money they made was usually plowed back into travel and equipment expenses. Many of these bands were very, very good—easily as good, or sometimes better, than the bands that we all heard on the radio. The reasons for not making it big sometimes had nothing to do with the music.

There were lots of opportunities for aspiring artists. Record companies had staffs of A&R (Artist & Repertoire) people, who were constantly on the lookout for the next big stars. In Hollywood, you only had to be good enough, not great. After that threshold was reached, many other factors became more important. To start off with, you had to be lucky. But most important was who you knew, or rather who knew you. The "right" names could open doors that sometimes weren't even visible. After the doors were opened and discussions centered around money, it was crucial for a new band to be willing to turn over all future revenue to the record label.

The major companies held all the cards. If a band was fortunate enough to get a recording contract, the record company would pay a small amount upfront for the band to live on while they cut their first album. Often the producer (who was assigned by the label) maintained artistic control and would determine what the band would sound like on their album. This was not always how the musicians wanted to sound, but the label had all the control— there was no contractual recourse.

The record company paid all recording costs including the purchase of new equipment if needed. If the record company was happy with the finished product, it may decide to distribute the album and push for airplay. Not all albums were promoted. Some were shelved for any number of reasons: the record company may have found a more promising prospect, the A&R guy or producer may have left the company, the graphics may not have been approved, may have gone over budget in production, or many other unpredictable reasons. Hopefully the shelving would be temporary, but sometimes it was indefinite.

If it was decided that the band was worth promoting, the record label would arrange to pay for advertising and promotion to the radio stations, distribution to record stores, and setting up a tour. All expenses such as transportation, lodging and other requirements of a touring band were fronted by the record company. Our hypothetical band is now on the road, playing second line to major acts with occasional headline bookings, getting some airplay and LP sales. Revenue is coming in from ticket sales, royalties (airplay), and publishing (LP sales).

However, the record company has paid out a lot of money to get the band where they are, and they want their money back—first and off the top. The musicians get nothing until these upfront expenses are paid. Furthermore, contracts were heavily skewed for the benefit of the record labels, so that even when all the upfront expenses were repaid, contract terms usually required all royalty and publishing revenues to be paid to the record company for the duration of the contract or even longer.

That left these very talented musicians with only one source of income: live performances. So they had to go back on the road to make a living while at the same time having a contractual obligation to produce a required number of albums. Even if their first album was shelved, they still had to meet the contractual obligation for more albums unless the record company opted to release the musicians from their contract. If the band had decent album sales, they became an "established act" with a "track record." They were then able to negotiate a better deal on the next contract.

This is a true story about the Stuart Little Band from the San Joaquin Valley in Northern California who kept getting closer and closer to signing the elusive recording contract. It could easily be the story of the hundreds of bands who competed for attention in the marketplace but because of bad luck, bad timing, bad decisions, and bad advice were never able to make that quantum leap to the next level.

We loved playing our music and being a part of the scene. It was an exciting and challenging time. We were dedicated to our success and to each other, forming a family bond and reaching for a goal that could only have been possible if we all made it the most important part of our young lives. If we had not tried our best to reach stardom, for the rest of our lives we would have asked ourselves, "What if…?"

This was truly a magical time for musicians…especially for a band called Stuart Little.

David Hoiem, San Francisco
Auguat 2015

Chapter 1: Purple Metalflake Hearse

Look upon the new day
You know what comes your way is somethin' new

—*Travelin' Song, Scott Liggett*

Peering back more than forty years through the wrong end of a telescope, it appears that a significant turning point in the Stuart Little Band was reached when Terry, our meth-head roadie, ran the purple metalflake hearse loaded with band equipment into the back of the third-hand limo that our drummer, Perry, had bought to chauffer us from gig to gig. A very intense confrontation ensued. Soon afterwards Perry, the drummer, abandoned his dream to be a rock star and left the band to pursue his other dream. He wanted join the U.S. Air Force and fly all over the world. We decided to keep playing anyway…after all, who needs a drummer to play rock music?

It was 1969, my freshman year at the University of the Pacific in Stockton, California when I joined the band. Most of the band members were students at UOP. Perry and Steve were enrolled at the College of the Pacific, where Steve was a psychology major and Perry studied counseling and experimental psychology. Grode was a philosophy major at Callison College. The Conservatory of Music at UOP is very well respected for its classical music curriculum, where Phil, Scott, and I attended. Phil was a voice major, Scott (who joined the band later) studied theory and composition, and I was a flute major. David K. and Bernie attended San Joaquin Delta College, located across the street. I don't know the background of Terry the Roadie. He was not very communicative because he was usually on his way up or down from a meth high.

In an attempt to create a mystical aura, we performed in hooded monk's robes. That was fine with me because I was trying to grow my hair out and the hood hid Perry's crewcut. My first gig was at the Sacramento Convention Center. We were the warm-up for HP Lovecraft and Bo Diddley. In addition to Perry on drums, Steve played bass, Grode harmonica, David K. lead guitar, Phil rhythm guitar and lead vocals, and I was on sax and flute. David K. and Steve sang lead vocals, too. We had a good reception and wrapped up our set with a big jam number called "California Zephyr." David sang lead and everybody had a solo (mine on sax, channeling Charles Lloyd very poorly.) I listened to the recording of that song 40 years later and edited out my embarrassing solo.

After the show, Bo Diddley approached us in the dressing room. "Man, you guys are somethin' else," he told us. "You have a special sound. I think I could help you out."

"You really think so?" I asked.

"Oh yeah. You guys are gonna go places. I can help you out."

" How can you do that?" questioned Steve and Phil almost simultaneously.

"I been playin' a long time. I got lots of contacts in the business. You guys should cut a record."

We all nodded our heads in agreement. We waited…

"Here's my card. Gimme me a call and we'll get something going."

I was in a daze. Things seemed to be going so fast. I had been in the band only a few months and here we were already talking record deals. We left to load our equipment in the purple hearse.

"Wow! Can you believe that?"

"Yea. This could be our big break."

Perry was, as usual, down to earth. "Are you guys going to believe that hype? He's bullshitting us just to make himself look important. You'll never get anywhere with him."

We countered Perry's comments with, "What if it's for real?" or "What makes you think he's lying? He sounds sincere to me."

We swallowed every word. We never heard from him again, even after several attempts to contact him. It would be some time before we realized that empty promises were a normal part of the music business. But we knew we had something special and unique. We just needed more exposure.

Phil had a friend who was a minister at a church in Stockton. He gave us a key to the outside entrance of the basement

3

and allowed us to use the space for rehearsal and equipment storage. It was very convenient because, in addition to allowing access at any time of the day or night, it was relatively soundproof and we could practice whenever the upstairs was not in use. It even had a small stage where we could leave our stuff set up between sessions. Because we all lived in Stockton the location was ideal.

For the next year or so, we continued on autopilot— rehearsing, working in new material, playing a few coffeehouses and clubs nearby, but not really going anywhere. We were really building our repertoire and refining our style. I was phasing out the sax in favor of the flute which was becoming more important in our sound; not only as a solo instrument but as another harmony line blending with the vocals. We incorporated elements of jazz, classical, folk, and country. Three and four part harmonies, dynamics, rhythm and key changes, and counterpoint were important parts of our sound. Grode, Phil, David K., and especially Steve were bringing a bunch of new material to practice sessions, where we improvised and experimented until we were satisfied that we had another piece that could be included in our set lists.

We had been doing some recording in a studio at KUOP, the University of the Pacific radio station, and Gold Star Studio in Los Angeles. We used these tapes to get some gigs locally and even got bookings at a couple small nightclubs in Los Angeles. We started making semi-frequent trips to L.A. to try and attract attention from record labels.

We generated a little bit of interest from one or two record companies. They sprang for more studio time so we could cut demo tapes. The experience was great and we made some good recordings.

The drive from Stockton to L.A. took about eight hours. We made the trip dozens of times without incident, but there were a couple instances that stuck in my memory. One night we were heading to Los Angeles and were south of Fresno on Highway 99. In 1969-1970 the highway was only one or two lanes in each direction and not a freeway, as it is today. It was probably around 9 or 10 o'clock when Steve looked to the side of the road and saw a car lying on its side down an embankment, with the wheels still turning.

"Perry, pull over!" he yelled.

"What? Why? What for?"

"Just stop right now! Look at that car! Down the side!"

Perry stopped and Steve led us down the embankment to the overturned car. We could see people inside. Perry went back to the limo to retrieve a tire iron and Terry got one from the hearse. Perry, Terry and I climbed up on the side of the car and began working on the doors. We were able to get the driver side door open and helped the couple out of the car. They seemed to be OK so after they thanked us we got back in our cars and continued on our way.

On another occasion, heading back to our cheap motel in L.A. after a late gig, we came across another wreck. This time it was a high performance car, maybe a Camaro or Firebird. It had gone off the exit ramp at high speed and was wrapped halfway around a light pole on the passenger side. There were two guys trapped inside. Once again, we got out the tire irons and pried the driver's door open. He was able to get out but his passenger was hurt, stuck, or both. We waited until the police arrived, then left when they were finished with us and an ambulance showed up.

Late one night as we were leaving a diner in L.A. Terry, driving the purple metalflake Cadillac hearse, rear-ended Perry's black Cadillac limousine. We were returning to Stockton after finishing a gig. The day before we had met with a record company to review the demo tapes that they had paid for. We thought the demo session turned out well and we were hoping to open contract negotiations.

We stopped at a diner to get a bite to eat before beginning the long trek back to Stockton. We had to stop to eat because Perry was very particular about his car. Not only was it always clean and shiny, he had an unbreakable rule: no eating, drinking, smoking or dirty shoes inside. As we were exiting the parking lot, Perry stopped his limo in the exit, waiting for traffic to clear. Then…BAM! Terry, driving the hearse, did not notice the stopped limo and rear-ended Perry's car, bending the bumper and trunk lid. Perry, very pissed off, jumped out to check the damage.

"What the hell are you doing? Can't you see that I was stopped?"

Terry was hopped up on uppers for the second or third consecutive day and was belligerent and almost out of control. "Just shut up man. I didn't do it on purpose. It was an accident. You shouldn't have stopped there."

"Look at that. You wrecked my car."

"I told you man, it was an accident. That's nothing…"

Perry was getting angrier, "I had to stop. You should pay attention to where you're going."

Terry became more aggressive. I could see it quickly escalating, so I tried to get in between and calm things down. "Terry, we know it was not on purpose," I said calmly. "I know you haven't slept much the past couple days. I can drive the hearse back and you can rest."

That really set him off. "Forget it! It's my car!" (It was partially his, the band had paid for half). "I can drive just fine and I don't need your help. Just get out of my way." Then he pulled out his ever-present Bowie knife and began waving it around in my direction, which convinced me that it was the end of the discussion.

Steve, Grode and Phil, in the meantime, had managed to calm Perry down. He was able to open the trunk, which was loaded with equipment. One of the microphone stands had been in the path of damage and was bent. We used that bent microphone stand for years afterwards. Then we all climbed back in the limo for the long, silent ride back to Stockton.

It was not long afterwards that Terry took the hearse and left for parts unknown, then Perry decided that his future lay with the U.S. Air Force and not a hippie rock and roll band.[*] Perry was such a perfect drummer for us that we were unable to find a replacement of his caliber. We were definitely at loose ends but didn't want to give up.

Unfortunately, without Perry, the energy slowly drained out of us like helium diffusing from a party balloon. We couldn't figure out what to do next so we kept doing what we had been doing, but the magic was not there. I moved back to my family home in Santa Rosa to work for my dad and commuted to Stockton on weekends for practice sessions, sleeping on a mattress on the floor of Phil's living room. Scott continued his pursuit of a degree in Theory and Composition, Steve completed his Master's degree in Psychology, Grode went back to school to finish his degree in Philosophy and I returned to my flute studies. Phil played solo coffee house gigs and Steve kept writing songs. Bernie continued his mime, performing at coffee houses, schools, and wherever he could get any kind of work. We didn't miss Terry, the meth-head roadie, but we did miss the purple hearse.

---

* Perry told me many years later that he didn't leave because of the accident, but that he had to make a choice between flying or playing music.

Chapter 2: Ending to Overture

Maybe in the morning light
We'll face a new tomorrow

—Times of My Life, Steve Solari

1970 was a very good year. We'd had some pretty good gigs lately, including the big outdoor concert at Pacific Memorial Stadium where we played warm-up up for the Byrds with a special guest appearance by Santana. We were getting regular work in a lot of nightclubs around the Valley and the San Francisco Bay Area. Our name was getting out there so that we were able to schedule dates without having to beg for a chance to play. We no longer had to play for "exposure" but actually got paid regularly although it wasn't very much. Our performances were getting tighter and our repertoire expanding. We had a few recordings that we were happy with. Things were definitely on the upswing. Although we knew it would be hard we could see a possible path to fame and fortune.

In those days, when a band was hired for a nightclub they were expected to be the entertainment for the entire night, from about 9:30 to last call. We had to play 3-4 sets without repeats. Our repertoire of 50-60 songs had taken a lot of work to put together, especially since everything was original except for two or three covers. Steve was writing a lot of the material, and Grode, Phil, and David Kemp were also making contributions. Perry and I didn't write but we had a lot of input during rehearsals as to the arrangements of our songs.

Playing in the Stuart Little Band was a six-way marriage. There was no alpha male leader. Decisions were made by consensus. It wasn't an easy way to reach agreement but our leaderless cohesion worked to create a unique and identifiable style.

One night, coming back from a nightclub in Sacramento, we were all tired from the gig and from loading equipment. We were laughing and joking as we climbed into Perry's limo. Cruising south on Highway 99, Perry was driving and the rest of us were stretched out in the back, semi-comatose, when Perry dropped a bombshell. "Hey guys, I hate to do this, but I'm going to have to quit the band."

We were stunned. David K. started laughing, "Yea, right" He assumed it was another of Perry's jokes. But Perry wasn't laughing.

"Are you serious, man?" asked Phil.

"C'mon, you're joking," chimed in Steve.

"Quit pullin' my leg," said Grode. "That's not even funny."

"Yea, get real," I said. "We need you. Things are lookin' good for us."

"Sorry guys. I really do have to leave. You know my dad is not well and I need to take care of him and my mom. I'm going to join the Air Force."

We looked at each other. "He really means it."

"I don't believe it. What are we going to do?"

"This sucks…"

We began to raise our voices. "C'mon Perry, you can't do this…"

"It's not even funny..."

We got louder. "Perry, you can't do this to us."

"Where will we find another drummer as good as you?"

"Knock it off, we know you're joking."

The comments became louder and more heated, so Perry just rolled up the privacy screen between the driver and passenger compartments. Of course, this just pissed us off so we started banging our fists against the glass and yelling.

He rolled it back down. "What do you guys want?"

"We want you to stay in the band."

"Yea, don't leave us now."

"Sorry guys, I've made my decision. It's been great but I need to move on. I've already been accepted at Officer Training School in the Air Force and I start real soon."

Once again we bombarded him with a growing chorus of complaints, so he raised the window again. Of course, we promptly began hammering on the glass with our fists and yelling. After a few minutes of this, he lowered the window again.

"Will you knock it off? I can't turn back now."

"But Perry, we can make it big."

"We have a chance. We just need to keep on with what we're doing." Our remarks continued coming faster and louder until once again he closed the window. Of course, we started banging and yelling again, but he refused to acknowledge us. The privacy screen stayed up until we reached our rehearsal space at the church.

We began unloading our equipment and hauling it down the stairs to the church basement. "Look guys," said Perry, "I appreciate your concerns but the decision has been made."

From Phil, "But Perry…"

"Just knock off the complaints. I've made the commitment and I can't go back. I will play the next couple gigs but I have to report to basic training in three weeks. It's been fun. I'll miss you guys and wish you the best luck. You have a good thing going and you'll get along fine without me."

Our next rehearsal without drums sounded terrible. We were totally discouraged and knew we had to find another drummer—a very difficult proposition since all the drummers we knew would not fit our style. In the meantime, we had a lot of new material to work in, so we continued practicing and keeping our eyes open for a suitable replacement.

To our surprise, some of the new songs were starting to come together. I bought a couple tambourines to add some percussion. Our new sound was more jazzy and less rock-n'-roll. I was concentrating on using the flute both as a supplement to vocal harmonies and a lead instrument. A distinctive sound was developing, different from every other band we had ever heard.

Another result of Perry's departure was a change in the chemistry. Without Perry providing a levelheaded buffer to our sometimes emotional discussions, it was difficult to arrive at agreements. Moreover, Phil had decided that he should be the leader and was becoming more autocratic. This was causing a lot of tension in the rest of us. We resented his assuming the leadership role when we had never had one before. Rehearsals became shorter and less frequent. The gigs began to dry up. It was time for all of us to make some changes.

Steve and his brother were the third generation Solaris on their farm near Lodi, California. Steve was not happily following in his family's footsteps and becoming a farmer, but he was reluctantly becoming more involved with running the business. After receiving his Bachelor in Psychology degree, he put most of his energy into the band but now that it was unraveling, he decided he had to return to his studies and get a Master of Psychology degree. This afforded him an activity away from the farm as well as the pursuit of a career goal.

Grode, too went back to UOP. He returned to Callison College to complete his degree in Philosophy. Callison was a liberal arts school with a focus on sensitivity towards non-Western studies including yoga, Zen, and Buddhist thought. As a part of the curriculum he was required to spend a semester or two in a third world country. After prepping at Callison College he went to Mazatlan for two semesters. We pretty much lost touch with him during his time away. This trip proved to be a major influence in his life, not all of it good.

Phil was married, with a little girl. He already had a part-time job at a music store in Stockton. He increased his hours so he could take care of his family. He continued playing solo appearances in local coffee houses.

David K. was also married, with a little boy. He could not conceive of doing anything but play music, so he formed a band with a friend of his. David K. played lead guitar, Scott Liggett on rhythm guitar, and a bass player. The trio was called Jenny Lind, named after the small town in the foothills where Scott lived.[*] They did a lot of acoustic music, playing around Stockton and the neighboring Sierra foothills.

I moved back to my parents' house in Santa Rosa, California and began working for my dad in his photofinishing business. The work was really boring but the pay was pretty good. I eventually bought a second-hand Mustang and moved to an in-law apartment near where I worked. My main activities were hanging out with friends and doing yoga. I really missed playing in the band and kept practicing my flute.

---

[*] The town was named after a famous singer who toured the Mother Lode during the 1849 gold rush.

We couldn't let go of the dream. We kept in touch with each other (except for Grode, who was in Mazatlan) and continued rehearsing and working up new material. Phil, Scott, and I were classically trained at the UOP Conservatory of Music. We reasoned that classical music does not need drums or percussion— the rhythm is an integral part of the music. So we decided to give up on our search for a drummer. Steve bought an Ovation fretless bass to replace his Epiphone bass because it had more punch. We set up a rehearsal schedule that was mostly on weekends so we could keep the band alive while working our day jobs.

I commuted to Stockton on Friday nights, and crashed during the weekend on a mattress on Phil's living room floor before returning to my job in Santa Rosa late on Sunday. We still had access to the church for practice space. In spite of our best efforts for several months, the magic never reappeared. Phil became more frustrated and demanding, new material was drying up. Steve's studies were exacting more time, and I was getting tired of the weekend commute. Eventually it all fizzled out and we went our separate ways. The future of the Stuart Little Band did not look promising.

People generally say, "You're so lucky to have a talent for music." At that time I would have agreed but I don't look at it that way now. Now I would say you have the curse of talent. Music was ingrained in all our souls and we couldn't give it up. I had grown increasingly unhappy with having a steady job, bills to pay and no outlet for my music. I quit my job and sold my car.

15

Steve and I continued to stay in touch, so I asked him if I could get a job on his farm. This was the summer of 1971. His brother hired me to drive a tractor and do other farm labor jobs. The Solari family let me set up a tent behind the family home under a huge, ancient walnut tree next to the old abandoned barn. They let me use the shower in the house when I needed it, which was every day. The work was hard and very dirty, but I liked it and enjoyed living in my tent. I eventually bought a bicycle and regularly pedaled into Stockton to hang out with friends when I wasn't working.

Steve had completed his Master's degree and was subsequently admitted into the doctoral program at the University of Utah in Salt Lake City. During the summer before he went to Salt Lake City he and I often hung out in my tent jamming; Steve on acoustic guitar and me on flute. Steve was still writing a bunch of new stuff. The style was very different from what we had previously done. More folk and jazz influence, but the songs were about life in the Central Valley and, of course, lost love.

One day he showed up with a new song. "What do you think of this? I don't have any words yet." He played some up-tempo cord changes.

"I really like it. Play it again." We were laughing a lot because the song just made us feel good.

I listened again and came up with a melody, light and tripping. We went through it a few times, congratulating each other on coming up with something we liked—still no words or name.

Suddenly I had an inspiration. "Steve! You know what this sounds like? It sounds like an overture to something...an opera."

Chapter 3: Opera from the Dust

The bow was drawn and the arrow let fly
Ravel's life had begun

—The Legend, Gordon Clark

"You're right. I know we can do it. We can write an opera. But what about?"

"Life on the farm, of course," I replied.

"Hmmm… that's great." We were getting excited. "A poor farm boy…"

"Yea. An immigrant who plays the flute…"

We thought about that while we played a couple more tunes.

I asked Steve. "What should we name him? We need some kind of generic ethnic name, not José or Rafael but something that's not specifically identifiable."

"Ravel," he answered.

"Love it. That's perfect." We were on a roll. The story line was evolving. We added a love interest, a tragedy, and a quest. We found we could use some of our existing material to support the unfinished story line but then we got stuck.

Grode had returned from Mexico, so we told him about our idea and played some of the songs. He really liked it and became as energized as we were. "Grode," I said. "We need to have some sort of third person viewpoint—an omniscient observer who can comment on the action."

Steve added, "And the story line is incomplete. You have any ideas?"

Grode nodded his head slowly and stared silently into the distance, or perhaps deep inside his head. This was something we had never seen in him before. He was usually upbeat and spontaneous, not slow-paced and introspective. It was the first of many changes we noticed in him since returning from Mazatlan.

After a couple minutes he pronounced, "The Logic Crow." And then he laughed out loud.

"What's the Logic Crow," I asked.

"He's a sort of shaman in the form of a crow. He flies overhead and not only observes what's going on, but takes part in it. He sees everything including the future."

"Wow, that's cool," said Steve.

I just nodded my head in agreement and rolled another joint. As I went to light it, Grode said, "Please don't do that. I can't stand to be around drugs."

"Really? You used to do this a lot."

"Not anymore, so please don't. It really affects my head."

"OK. We're still missing parts of the story line. Any ideas?"

We brainstormed for a couple hours and came up with a rough idea—enough to start adding music from our repertoire. There were a bunch of gaps in the music, so we needed a lot of new material.

"I can write some poetry," said Grode.

"And I can come up with some ideas for new songs," added Steve.

"I'll work on the story line," I said. "It needs to flow better and we need to incorporate Grode's poems."

Ravel
The Unraveling
(A Ballet In Mime)

It was a sunny day many, many years ago when I first met Ravel. He was sitting under an old oak tree standing near a small creek. A gypsy by birth and an orphan, he worked long hours in the peat fields. His youthful face was filled with the weight of many hard years and yet in the distance I could hear faint traces of music. Perhaps it was the light in his eye, perhaps it was the wink and nod of his laughter, I cannot say. Nonetheless I did not see Ravel again for many a day.

It was upon my return that Ravel first approached me. His wings were young and one could see deep within his heart that he was struggling for flight. Standing before me, he humbly paused and then lifting his dark sad eyes he asked a boon. I accepted and with that the legend was sewn.

For many a month I taught Ravel the way of music—to call the young sparrow, to carry the drift of the morning breeze, and to breathe with the river of life itself. We would sit among the early morning sundogs and Ravel would play his wooden flute while

Suskia, his childhood sweetheart, would sit and listen beaming like the morning sun itself.

Years passed and Ravel grew to be a young man. His time had come to master the task of music. He took up his life savings, hung a brown tote bag from his shoulder, and with flute in hand set out for the University. After several months of ardent study, Ravel performed his first recital . . . "La Dance Pour une Nuit des Tempêtes." He received an instantaneous standing ovation: a crowning moment for a man so young. It was in the midst of joy and laughter that his tears turned to sadness . . . Suskia was dead.

For days he floundered in grief and sorrow. Life had lost all meaning. Finally, with tear filled eyes, he packed his bags and returned to the fields of home. He had given up his life's work. It grieved me greatly to see him tumbling so, a man of so much love.

Slowly the seasons passed. It was in the autumn when the leaves turn that Ravel had a dream. Before him stood his old friend the flute master. His beard was still of silver, his eyes of deepest blue, and in his outstretched hands he held a lovely golden flute. As the vision faded a voice, like a gentle wind deep within his heart spoke forth, "Follow the way of music, Ravel . . . follow the way of music."

The next day Ravel wandered along the little winding creek until he came to the old oak tree of his youth. There he sat among the early morning sundogs contemplating his life and its mysteries. Suddenly a crow called loudly overhead. He looked up and there beheld a golden aura emanating from a lovely flute. Climbing the tree, he lifted the flute from its resting place and played the first notes since Suskia's death. Tears were streaming from his eyes, his face shining with the light of love.

Shortly thereafter, Ravel returned to his studies and mastered the flute. And, as the years passed he illuminated the four corners of the world with the beauty of his song. With age came wisdom and the completion of a life's work. The geese have flown to heaven.

The Logic Crow
Synopsis of "Ravel" as written by Grode

We wanted to re-form the band, but the specter of Phil was haunting us. His operatic voice and overbearing demeanor was unpalatable. Grode, Steve, and I decided we should contact David Kemp and see if he wanted to work on "Ravel" with us. His electric lead guitar and impeccable phrasing would be an integral part of our sound. He agreed to try it, so we met in Steve's garage and explained in more detail, then ran through the material that we had pinned to the story. We could feel the magic returning. He really liked the idea of starting over, but said he couldn't work with Phil. I agreed. This was not a style where Phil would fit and we didn't want him taking charge.

Steve had started the band with Phil in 1968, so it was very hard for him to leave Phil out at this time. However, he could see which way we were leaning, and had to agree that the style was totally different than anything we had done two years earlier. He reluctantly agreed to do "Ravel" without Phil. So now we had four: David Kemp on lead guitar and vocals, Steve Solari on bass and vocals, Gordon Clark on harmonica and vocals, and me on flute and light percussion. Drums would have been good, but our search was fruitless. We needed a rhythm guitar.

"Scott," said David K.

"Who's Scott?" I asked.

"Scott Liggett. I play with him in Jenny Lind. He's really good and has a great voice."

Steve wanted to practice again in a couple days. "See if he can come. I'd like to meet him."

At the next session, Scott came carrying an acoustic guitar. That was a good sign in itself as we were not loud. We practiced without a PA or microphones. Later when we performed live, we even wore earplugs on stage to protect our hearing. A comment we often got from the audience was, "Turn it up!" We didn't.

We couldn't believe what was happening. Scott was instantly in tune with our sound and immediately embraced the concept of "Ravel." He and Steve joined forces to become our rhythm section. His voice complemented the vocals and his easy-going personality was a direct contrast to Phil. The missing drummer was no longer a concern.

It was a very dramatic scene in Steve's garage when we let Phil know that we no longer wanted him in the band. He couldn't believe that we were serious and he took it very hard when it finally sank in. He walked up to Scott, glared at him, and then slapped him across the face before storming out. We had a new band and a new sound. We were going to go places.

Chapter 4: Barstools and Whiteface

Maybe I'll play my guitar
And write a song

—*Sunset Sunrise, David Kemp*

Bernie Bang had been performing with the Stuart Little Band pretty much from the beginning, when we wore monk's robes on stage. He was naturally talented and worked very hard at the classical art, keeping the ancient theater tradition of mime alive. The art form is very physically demanding and Bernie was in excellent physical condition, very likely the strongest person I have ever met. Definitely the best mime I have ever seen, even in some ways better than Marcel Marceau. His movements brought everything to life. When he held a glass of water and drank it, you could see the imaginary glass. Throwing a ball, flying a kite, climbing through a window to burglarize a home, eating a meal, and dozens of other skits were done so well that you could almost see the props created by his movements and expressions, which were, of course, only in your imagination.

In 1970 Bernie went to Paris to study at the Marcel Marceau School of Mime. He was there eleven months and honed his skills to an astonishing level. When he returned in 1971, traditional mime in whiteface makeup was still a relatively obscure form of theater in the United States. It wasn't until a year or two later that a dropout from the Marcel Marceau School of Mime named Robert Shields began street performances at Union Square in San Francisco. He became well known for doing the "mechanical man," "shrinking glass box," and imitating people on the sidewalk, but not much else. I attribute his prostitution of the art for the creation of the public perception of a whiteface mime as a running joke.

We were glad to have Bernie back to perform with us. He became "Ravel." As we began a few performances in small venues he performed in front of us while we sat on tall stools. We were a very laid back group on stage, so Bernie provided visual focus. As the opera became more polished we began playing more and more in nightclubs and bars. Because "Ravel" was only two sets, about an hour and a half of music, we had to bring in our other material to fulfill our obligation to play for the entire evening. We would usually start with a set of songs we knew well, and throw in one or two new ones that we were working on so we could gauge public reaction. Then, we would wind up the evening with "Ravel." This format worked very well for us and we continued with it until we had enough other material to play all night without having to perform "Ravel" in its entirety. Bernie was not always with us, but he joined us on stage when we had a "big gig."

Ron Schwartz was a long-time fan and another UOP student. He really liked us and saw a lot of potential in our music.

One day he showed up at practice at the Solari farm driving a blue and white Volkswagen microbus. It had little oval windows around the roofline, a sunroof, and flowered curtains in all the side windows. He had traded in his American muscle car for this hippiemobile. He made us an offer. "I want to be a part of what you're doing. I'll haul your equipment and set up bookings for you guys if you let me join you."

"Let's talk this over," Steve said to us. "In private."

We discussed the pros and cons. We needed transportation for our equipment. We had been using the Solari farm's old white pickup when the farm workers didn't need it, but it was getting late in the season and would start raining soon. We also were not very good at getting bookings, and needed to play in more places and make more money. Ron seemed to fit the bill for both, but none of us knew him real well so we were hesitant to bring in another band member, especially an unknown personality. But he was offering us something that we really needed. On the other hand, we would be splitting our pay six ways instead of five.

"OK, Ron. We'll take a chance," pronounced Steve, our kind of default spokesman. "But no guarantees. If it doesn't work out, we dissolve the arrangement."

We all shook on it and waited to see what would happen. To our surprise, Ron started coming through with new and better gigs. Our pay was usually the cover charge and a percentage of the bar. The band sometimes made $200-$300 a night. Most of the gigs were for one or two nights, sometimes more.

We were playing a lot, and in a lot of different places. Not every venue was a good fit, but that made them memorable. In San Francisco, we were playing at a lesbian bar that was rather small and dark. We were splitting the bill with Big Joe Williams, alternating sets. He played a unique old-style country blues. Instead of the usual 12-bar blues with four beats per measure, he didn't count measures or beats. Sometimes they were 9, 11, 13, or whatever-bar blues, with any number of beats per measure. Chord changes were seemingly random.

One young lady attracted Steve's attention, so he started putting the move on her. Her girlfriend was not happy with this. Suddenly, "CLICK! " she had a switchblade in her hand and very quietly told Steve, "Leave the bitch alone or I'll cut off your nuts." Steve took her suggestion to heart.

In about the middle of the third set with Big Joe playing and stomping his foot, a very angry woman walked in and accused the bartender of cheating on her. A loud argument ensued and then the patron produced a knife and started to climb over the bar. The bartender was not intimidated. She reached under the bar and grabbed a revolver which she pointed at her aggressor and slowly cocked. Nobody was injured and the stalemate ended when the cops showed up and removed the patron. These were some very tough ladies indeed.

Another unusual gig was in King City, California. This is a small rural town, about 150 miles south of San Francisco on Highway 101. It is in the middle of nowhere in redneck country.

27

Ron had booked us into a country-western bar for one night. Walking into the bar to set up, we all stopped, stunned, and stared at the room. "Is this for real?" I asked the guys. Ron had made the booking over the phone and had never seen the place.

We looked around in astonishment. Wagon wheel chandeliers were hanging from the exposed beams and bison heads kept guard above the bar. Framed guns and rifles and cowboy photos were posted on the walls. But the most amazing part of the room was the stage, dead center in the middle of the room and completely surrounded by eight foot tall chicken wire fencing. It was a real life scene from the movie, "The Blues Brothers." So we opened the gate, hauled our equipment in and set it up. We knew "Ravel" was not an option.

Showtime: We walked on stage—five long-haired hippies—sat down on our stools and tuned up. There were about 100 or more cowboys in the audience, complete with Stetson hats, pointy-toed boots and smoking like crazy. The lights came up and we started with our usual first song; the Overture from "Ravel," which is mostly a kind of bouncy flute solo. The words are "la-la-la-la." After a long silence from the crowd, the place went nuts. Beer bottles, peanuts, and ashtrays came flying at the stage, bouncing off the chicken wire. We finished the song. David K. said, "Maybe we should do the theme from "Rawhide" for the rest of the night." We didn't know it. We had a couple country-western type songs, so we rolled those out and things got a little calmer. We tried to stay with our more rock 'n' roll type songs for the rest of the set, which were met with only a handful of flying beer bottles.

We took a break and went back up there. By that time, the crowd had thinned quite a bit. We played four or five songs and then the manager came to us and told us we might as well stop playing. They still paid us, but it wasn't much, maybe $100 or a little more. We packed up and left. After that we asked Ron to check out the venues a little more before booking us.

There was a biker bar on 4th St. in San Rafael. We had been booked there before. They must have liked us because they brought us back. It was a pretty rough and tumble place with about an inch of peanut shells on the floor from the freebies handed out at the bar. The crowd was typical bikers, with tattoos, leather vests, unkempt facial hair and rowdy. We were playing our usual stuff and things seemed pretty normal. It was a pretty full house.

Everybody was drinking and some were dancing. Midway in the second set a ruckus broke out by the front door. We couldn't tell exactly what was happening but it started getting pretty loud. And then, CRASH! The bouncer, who weighed at least two hundred pounds, came flying butt first through one of the large plate glass windows into the bar. The guy that threw him, probably weighing three hundred pounds, followed him inside through the window then jumped on him. As the customers began taking up

29

sides and forming alliances, I picked up a microphone stand and was ready to swing it at anybody who came near the stage. Then David K. opened the back door of the stage, which was an exit to the alley in the rear of the bar. We all slipped out with our instruments and waited until things calmed down.

Upon re-entering, there were still a lot of people there, so we kept playing. Eventually someone showed up with a sheet of plywood and nailed it over the broken window. We got back on our stools and finished our sets. The rest of the night was quiet.

Chapter 5: Grode's Playhouse

Sittin in my shack, listenin' to the wind,
Blowin' so cold 'gainst my window pane
.

—*Blue Fox, Gordon Clark*

Summer of 1971 was nearing its end and it was harvest season on the farm. Peaches and cherries were packed and gone, the walnut trees were being shaken, the bean harvester was getting readied for another season, and winter wheat was getting planted. It was getting too cold for me to sleep in my tent under the giant walnut tree by the old barn, so Grode allowed me to move in with him for a short time. We were on the road a lot, so oftentimes nights were spent in cheap motels where one of us rented a single room and everybody else sneaked in with sleeping bags.

The sleeping arrangements were a source of tension among our tight-knit family. I often insisted on taking either the mattress after removal to the floor, or else the box spring, which stayed on the bedframe. Sometimes I lost my argument and had to sleep on the floor, which made me cranky and I asserted I could not play as well. Also, Grode's newly discovered aversion to drugs was somewhat antithetical to our lifestyle of "drugs, sex, and rock 'n' roll." We weren't into a lot of drugs, but we did smoke weed. If we lit up in the room, Grode would get very upset and ask us to take it outside. We sometimes refused him and suggested that he leave. At that point he argued (correctly, I might add) that the smell would still be in the room and it messed with his head.

In any case, Grode allowed me to move in with him after reaching an agreement that I would not smoke in his quarters. He was renting a small cottage, more of a playhouse—maybe 150 square feet—located in the back yard of one of his professors from Callison College. Bathroom and kitchen were in the main house. There was a bed, a small table, and a sort of counter under which I spread my sleeping bag. Our bicycles were also kept inside. Very cozy, but it kept out the rain.

Grode was pretty reclusive and I didn't know him very well. I'm not sure any of us did. His father was a famous neurosurgeon from the Mayo Clinic and lived in a rather exclusive community of homes that were built on Federal parkland with a 99-year lease above Muir Beach in Marin County. His sister, Susan, lived at home while Grode went to school and traveled with the band. In spite of coming from a somewhat privileged background, Grode had very simple tastes and was not at all ostentatious. Quite the opposite, in fact. For example, when he decided he needed a car, instead of picking up the BMW from his parents' house, he found a faded blue ancient Studebaker Lark that was somehow still running. He dressed in overalls, tennis shoes, and flannel shirts. You could spot him a mile away. His tall, lanky figure, somewhat stooped and his usually unkempt longish blond hair made him stand out in any crowd. His slow, shuffling gait made him seem like a seventy year old man trapped inside the body of a twenty-two-year old.

I wanted to get to know him better. He was so mysterious and so different from the Grode I knew before he went away. Before leaving for Mazatlan, he was usually ready with a laugh and some sort of odd insight into whatever we were discussing, oftentimes while passing a doobie. He would readily share his thoughts and private jokes. Most of the time we could follow his thinking, although, often as not, those thoughts would lead us into unexpected places. He was very intelligent and observant of people and things around him. Now, he was introspective, prone to long silences and very tired most of the time. He slept long hours and needed very regular meals or else he just, as he put it, "faded away."

One morning over our breakfast cereal I posed the question, "What was it like in Mazatlan?"

He put down his spoon and sat silently for several moments. Staring off into the distance, he answered me. "Hot. It was extremely hot."

"That's all? What did you do there?"

"I got really sick. I had a bad case of dysentery."

"What were the people like?"

"They were very, very poor. It was quite sad. I will never go back there."

33

"But why did you go?"

"It was for school."

And that was pretty much all I could get out of him. He remained silent until I changed the subject and talked about what we were working on at the time or an upcoming gig. Every time the subject of Mazatlan came up, he withdrew and refused to discuss it. We never knew what happened there that caused such a drastic personality change. Sometimes the old Grode broke through with a joke or an observation, but those moments were rare. He talked a lot about wisdom acquired in old age. It seemed to me that he wished he were older and wiser, rather than a young man in his early 20's.

Mysticism was an important part of his worldview. He talked of spirits, shamans, and other mystical beings that were a part of his life. He spent a lot of time with Jesse, a Mexican gardener at UOP, whom he claimed was a shaman and helped him gain insights into his life and the world surrounding him, both real and fantastical.

He was an active participant in all aspects of the band during the end of 1971 and early 1972. He came to all the practices and gigs, wrote songs, and joined us on the road. Later on, as he became more introverted, his energy was seeping away and he started begging off from some of our gigs. He usually joined us when we played "Ravel" but if it was just a regular nightclub gig he would sometimes join us and sometimes not.

After a couple months staying with Grode, I met a young lady at a friend's house. We hit it off and she offered to let me stay with her in Stockton while I was between gigs, so I moved out of Grode's playhouse.

Chapter 6: Synergy

Don't ask me why, it's hard to say
It may be love, may be just my way

—*Burn the Wind, Gordon Clark*

David Kemp had received no formal musical training but nevertheless he was an incredible musician. He could pick up any instrument with strings and make it sound good. He even doubled on flute when we wanted a second part. Born with one defective ear, he compensated by having perfect pitch and being able to quickly memorize lines and chord progressions. His solos were performed with almost mathematical precision, adhering to very structured 8-bar call-and-response phrases.

Very much a stickler for intonation, we always played in tune or faced his displeasure. There was one problem with his perfect pitch. At home he had a run-down phonograph with a turntable that turned slightly slow, so he was accustomed to hearing a pitch that was slightly below the standard concert A440 pitch. This did not create a problem for the other guys because they could tune their strings to match David's and we had no keyboard (which would have required using standard pitch). However, because I had to tune my flute almost a ¼ step low, it was difficult to play in tune because the instrument was built to the A440 standard. Changing the length of the tube required me to adjust each note differently than I would have if the instrument were tuned correctly. I once bought an A440 tuning fork and asked him to use it, but he said it was wrong and refused, so with some difficulty I made the changes, but not without grumbling when he complained that I was out of tune.

David was blessed with a high, clear voice and we often told him how good he sounded. He didn't believe us and always responded quite honestly, in his opinion, that he couldn't sing. He loved to write songs about transportation such as "Western Pacific," "California Zephyr," and "Greyhound Bus." "Sunset Sunrise" is a particularly beautiful ballad that wouldn't have been out of place on a Crosby, Stills and Nash recording.

He was very skinny and hyperactive with long fingers and a ready laugh. The main components of his diet were cigarettes and chocolate milk. He concealed his defective ear with big bushy, sandy-colored hair and wore a full beard, no mustache.

Because he was so very sensitive about his hearing loss, he wore earplugs for performances and insisted on very low volume for rehearsals. The rest of us also decided to protect our hearing and so we all wore earplugs when performing [*] even though we weren't very loud on stage. It wasn't unusual to get cries from the audience to "turn it up." Which of course, we ignored.

---

[*] None of us today have hearing problems caused by too much volume.

37

Although being one of the most talented musicians I have ever known, he had no business sense and just went along with whatever plans we made. As long as he could perform he was content and had no long-term goal other than to keep playing. How he paid his rent, supported his wife and son, and kept his 1959 Peugot 403 on the road was a mystery to me. He was not making any more money than the rest of us and of course he was always broke. It's possible that Mary, his wife, was working part-time and they were receiving some public assistance but I don't know that for a fact.

I am convinced that David K. feared success. He often made references to not wanting to "prostitute the music." He was concerned that we would "sell out" to big corporations and lose our identity. When asked about being rich and famous, he would reply that he didn't care so long as he could play his music.

Grode was not hard to pick out in a crowd. He had long, straight blond hair, fair complexion and a clean-shaven long face. He was over six feet tall with bright blue eyes that took in everything around him while giving the impression that he was detached from his surroundings, almost as if he was in a bubble. This invisible barrier was only a one-way screen. Able to focus intensely on events and circumstances around him, he absorbed these inputs and then processed them. Later, seemingly from nowhere, he would pronounce his observations and conclusions from a perspective that made me kind of scratch my head, think about it, and say to myself, "It probably would make a lot of sense if I could figure out what he's saying. It doesn't seem to be totally off-base, but still..." Much of his poetry and lyrics captured this feeling.

Just two years older than me, his perspective on life was that of an elder. He craved the wisdom that comes with age and spoke of it often. Many of his songs were written as if he were fifty years older. His singing style was consistent with advanced age. As time progressed after his return from Mazatlan, he moved deeper and deeper into this facsimile of agedness. His focus moved inward. His communication with us became more centered on philosophical observations and further from the outside world. Physically, he became weaker and more stooped. His participation in the band lessened and he came to fewer and fewer gigs because he was feeling worn out.

The Solari farm, located between Stockton and Lodi, was founded in the late 1800's by Steve's great-grandfather. When I drove tractor in the fields, Steve's dad, Stephen Sr., and his brother, Frank, ran it. Steve participated in family decisions, but otherwise was not involved in the daily operations. His grandmother also lived at the farm and recalled the days in the 1800's when she was a young girl riding a buckboard into Stockton for supplies. She was a very bright and sprightly lady who took everything in stride. It was amazing to me that she had lived from the days of plowing fields with horses to seeing an American astronaut on the moon.

The family was proudly Italian, 100% Genovese extraction. Steve's grandmother easily spoke English, but she and his parents spoke Italian with each other in private. They were a warm and loving family and welcomed all of us hippie musicians to their home in traditional Italian fashion. Any time one or more of us showed up we were ushered into the kitchen, where seemingly by magic, the table was covered with dishes of delicious homemade goodies. We had to eat or they would have had their feelings hurt. If we were leaving on tour or to L.A., they filled our gas tanks from the farm supply. The warmth and generosity of the Solari family set an undertone for all our music and business dealings. The farm was the incubator for the Stuart Little Band.

Steve was a little shorter than me, maybe 5'8" or 5'9" and average build. Dark eyed, with curly dark hair worn long as a "natural," sporting a full beard and mustache he very much displayed his Genovese heritage. Extremely generous, he did more than his share to support our endeavors, often fronting us cash when we were short for a trip to L.A., a needed motel room, or had to pay professional fees. We made every effort to promptly repay him. He was always willing to provide transportation in the "Green Hornet," his AMC Hornet station wagon that he had purchased to move us and our equipment.

One time, while I was in my tent on the farm I heard an airplane swooping low overhead. It was Steve flying a rented Cessna 150 buzzing me. What was really funny was that by the time he made a second pass all the farmhands had dropped their tools and ran as fast as they could for the cover of the trees. They thought he was "La Migra."

Steve's writing style was not typecast. His music included country, rock, blues, and ballads. These stylistic influences were a big part of creating the unique Stuart Little sound that was difficult to describe because we didn't fit a specific genre. Playing a fretless Ovation bass, he kept our rhythm steady and provided the drive that moved the music ahead. A prolific songwriter, he wrote more than half the material that we performed as well as singing lead and backup. He continues writing and producing his music today.

"Who lit the rope?" was often asked by David K. when Steve lit up one of his Swisher Sweets.

"What this country needs is a good five-cent cigar," Steve would reply, happily puffing away.

Staid and conservative in his dress, he was often ready for an adventure. One time we were staying at a cheap motel on Sunset Boulevard in L.A. and wanted to pursue a little excitement. Possession of marijuana was extremely illegal during that decade, but being true counter-culture members, we liked to yank the chain of "The Man" whenever we could. I had a plan.

"Let's roll up a doobie then head out to the Strip to smoke it and see how long it will take for the cops to bust us," I suggested. "Since we just have one, when they pull up, I'll swallow it and there will be no evidence."

"Are you crazy?" he asked.

"Yea, but it will be fun. We can't get in trouble if they don't find any weed," I replied.

"You guys are nuts," Scott declared.

David K. looked up from his guitar. "Don't ask us to bail you out."

"Great. Let's do it," agreed Steve.

"Steve, be sure you have your ID. They'll want to see it," I told him.

So we fired one up and stepped out on the sidewalk, passing it back and forth as we walked down the street, ostentatiously enjoying every hit. We'd made it a couple blocks when, with screeching tires, three police cars pulled up to the curb, red lights flashing, and out jumped five cops. I quickly extinguished the joint on my tongue and swallowed it. They rushed us, threw us against the wall, and started frisking us. Of course, they found nothing until they asked us to open our mouths.

"What's that?" one asked, peering into my mouth with a flashlight. "It looks like ashes."

"Yea," I answered. "I just ate some ashes."

"I bet you swallowed a joint. If we pumped your stomach we'd find one."

"I don't think you can do that without a search warrant."

They were really pissed off, but after running our licenses they couldn't do anything since they had no evidence. "We'll get you guys," they warned us as they left.

Back at the motel, Steve and I were a little shaken by the cops roughing us up but we had lots of good laughs when we related our experience.

All the girls liked Scott. He wore muttonchops, a mustache, and long brown hair tied into a ponytail. His ready smile and big brown "bedroom eyes" attracted a lot of feminine attention. He played a very energetic rhythm guitar and was usually drenched in sweat by the middle of the first set. His crooner's voice when he sang lead was a contrast to David K.'s simple tone and Steve's lower earthy timbre. The three part harmonies were just beautiful. I sometimes added a fourth part with my flute.

Scott was kind of a quiet guy with a warped sense of humor. He was the great peacekeeper. When conflicts started to get out of hand, he would calm everybody down and remind us of what we were trying to accomplish. He carefully considered the situation then made some sort of sarcastic comment about what was going on before stepping back to offer a common sense suggestion. I never saw him get mad. He was passionate about the music and the band and dedicated to making a successful musical career. Scott is the only one of us that actually made it happen.

He lived in the Sierra foothills in the little town of Mokelumne Hill and got us booked at the Hotel Leger a few times, one of which was an early performance of "Ravel" with kids and dogs running around at our feet.
Scott eventually traded his VW bug for a mustard colored Datsun pickup with a camper shell in which he traveled from home to gig.

He slept in the back with his girlfriend so he did not have to share a motel room with the rest of us.

Once, down in L.A., Scott suggested we go to a strip club. I had never been to one and thought it was a great idea to see some female flesh. Steve, Scott and I got in the Green Hornet and found a club on the Strip, paid our cover and went in. It was the usual kind of sleazy place—dimly lit, overpriced, watered-down drinks, and a big oval stage in the center with a couple poles and topless girls dancing in g-strings. There were a bunch of older businessman types sitting around the perimeter of the stage. I had no extra cash to throw to the dancing girls on stage so the topless waitresses received my attention. "Hey, let's sit back here," suggested Scott, pointing to a back table by the dressing room door.

"Cool," I said as I watched the girls go in and out. We picked up our drinks and moved into the dark corner. The girls, who were mostly our age, promptly took note of us.

"Why don't you guys go sit up there?" asked one, pointing to the stage.

"We like it here," said Scott.

"But you can see a lot better up there."

"I like what I see here," answered Steve.

"Yea," I chimed in. "We can't talk to you up there."

We stayed there for a couple hours and had a great time. There were always one or two girls standing around our table. They even bought us a round of drinks.

I had shoulder length brown hair with a full beard and mustache. I wore John Lennon oval eyeglasses and was of average height, about 5'10" and pretty slim. I was often told that I resembled the images of Jesus when he was portrayed as a Western European of Nordic heritage.

I was the youngest member and a bit of a prima donna. More often than not, I was responsible for conflicts because I was very stubborn and wanted more than anything to get rich and famous playing rock 'n' roll music. I dreamed of private jets, sailboats, limousines, and mansions. I was ready to do almost anything to make it happen and at times I became frustrated with the intransigence of my bandmates and couldn't understand why they didn't see it my way. When we started getting more recognition and more work in 1972 and 1973, I wanted us to work really hard. I thought we should practice every day and gig six times a week. We never met that schedule, which was a source of frustration to me.

During this same time period, I read a book (I was always reading books) by Arnold Ehret on the Mucusless Diet Healing System. The author advocated a fruitarian diet, consisting of only fruits and nuts, regular fasting, and no starches. The purpose was detoxification and improved health. I did not follow it exactly because I liked bread too much, and I'm sure that smoking weed was proscribed. The most significant effect was my dramatic weight loss from 160 lbs. I had grown fat from eating fondue and steak. I lost a lot of weight, getting down to 128 lbs. I could even fit in my girlfriend Debbie's pants. She weighed 110 lbs.

I loved all the music we performed. My writing skills were very limited so in that respect I did not contribute much. However, I was very active in arranging and strived for perfection in rehearsal. Sometimes I pushed too hard and the other guys told me to back off.

The band was originally formed when Steve and Phil came to Perry Karraker's door one day and asked if he would be interested in joining a band called Stuart Little. He liked that there was a mime and original material. He had just left another band and was willing to join a new band. Even though Perry was not active in Stuart Little after 1970, his absence continued to be an influence throughout the following years. We never found another drummer that could be a part of our sound.

Almost forty years later, Perry commented to me, "We all took something from the band that made us better people. Even in my military career I used the lessons from Stuart Little. We learned to respect each other and work together to make something happen that none of us could have done individually. It's been a big part of all our lives."

We were all so different, yet somehow managed to make this group marriage work and create something wonderful and bigger than we all were. We wanted to make a comfortable living or achieve stardom from our music. Life together was not all hugs and kisses—we had many very passionate disagreements through the years, but we all knew that we could not achieve what we wanted without each other. The love of music, especially our music, held us together and kept us pulling in the same direction until repeated failures and financial hardship drove us all to eventually pursue other life goals.

Chapter 7: Fantasy

Would a better man know right from wrong
Would he know to sing a better song

—*Better Man, Phil McKay*

The New Orleans House on San Pablo Avenue in Berkeley brought in all kinds of music, but more importantly for us, was not averse to giving local talent a chance to be heard. Charlie Musselwhite, Clover (which later became Huey Lewis and the News), Boz Scaggs, Tower of Power, Seatrain, Sopwith Camel, Quiksilver Messenger Service, Steve Miller Band, and many other well-known and local bands played there. We had our first performance there in October 1970 and quickly became regulars, steadily growing our audience. This was a great showcase and a chance to test new material. We became much tighter and more relaxed on stage, still sitting on tall stools while performing, although I would stand at a mike (barefooted if possible) when I played my lines. It was beginning to feel like we had a home base.

By the end of summer in 1971 we were ready to put on the premier performance of "Ravel." We had typed up the entire 16-page libretto with story line, poetry and lyrics. We wanted to pass this out to the audience to make it easier to follow. Steve and I went late one night to the UOP Library where there was a newly installed photocopy machine. We proceeded to run off about 20-30 copies, then collated and stapled them. There were no restrictions on the use of the machine, so we did this several more times until the school got wise to such heavy use and restricted access. In September 1971 we put on the premier with Bernie Bang miming the various roles. It was a huge success. We performed it multiple times thereafter, but soon ran out of librettos to hand out.

The greatest benefit of performing there was a member of the audience. The club's owner, Kitty, was a good friend of a prominent Bay Area jazz and pop music critic, Ralph Gleason. Not only was he the music critic for the San Francisco Chronicle, he was a founding editor of Rolling Stone magazine and cofounder of the Monterey Pops Festival. Even more important to us was the fact that he was a Vice President at Fantasy Records. Fantasy was attempting to expand their jazz portfolio to include more pop acts, adding Joe Walsh and John Fogarty to their stable of artists. Ralph Gleason liked us a lot, and came to hear us almost every time we played.

Steve somehow found out Ralph was diabetic, so offered to bring him a box of cherries from the farm. This turned into a meeting in his office. "I really like your music, but I don't think you're quite ready yet. I'd like to hear more. What can I do to help you?"

We were having a difficult time getting together to practice regularly. We were always welcome at the farm but we were scattered all over the place. Grode had moved back to Marin, Steve lived on the farm, Scott lived in Mokelumne Hill in the Sierra foothills, David K. was living with his in-laws in the Berkeley hills and I was mostly in Santa Rosa. "We could sure use a place to practice," we told him.

"Let me see what I can do."

He came through for us. Fantasy Records was located in the industrial flatlands of Berkeley. It was not a huge complex, but they had two or three practice studios that were accessible from the street. Ralph made arrangements for us to use one on weekends. We thanked him and set up a rehearsal schedule. On Friday afternoons, David K. came down to Fantasy Records and picked up the key to the practice room. The rest of us made our way there with our instruments and sleeping bags. We met at the studio, set up our equipment and practiced until we were too tired, then crashed on the floor. This continued all weekend until late Sunday, when we packed up and cleaned our mess in the studio. First thing Monday morning, David K. returned the key to the Security Office.

We worked up a lot of new material and really polished "Ravel." Ralph kept tabs on our progress and made arrangements for us to cut some demos in the recording studio. They turned out quite well. [*] We were getting some feelers from Fantasy about a recording contract. We entered serious discussions and then reached a major stumbling block. We wanted to keep some of the money that we could potentially be making.

In the 1970's there were a lot of bands getting signed and produced. It was a real boom time for the major record labels but smaller independents didn't have much of a chance because the big companies controlled most of the distribution channels. Another benefit for the labels was the plethora of bands competing for recording contracts. The A&R guys (Artists and Repertoire, essentially talent scouts) could pick and choose those that they thought would be most profitable for their company. The criterion was profit, not talent. The artists didn't have to be great, just good enough. It was even worse for the unknown bands with new contracts. They were mostly young guys with stars in their eyes, just like us. They knew nothing about the business other than that they wanted an album produced with their name and pictures. The boilerplate contracts presented by the record company attorneys turned over all rights to the company in exchange for producing and possibly, but not necessarily, distributing an album. The companies would then front money for a tour if they decided that they wanted to promote the album. The band would have to forego all revenue from the tour and LP sales until production and front

---

[*] The recording engineer was a very good drummer and laid some tracks on some of the demos. We asked him to join us, but he declined.

monies were reimbursed to the record company. Most bands made nothing on the road after expenses, but they usually had a good time, although as often as not ending up even deeper in debt.

Money from album sales came from two sources: publishing and royalties. When an album was sold at retail, fifty cents was paid to the publishing company, which was commonly owned by the record label. Royalties came from airplay on radio or television. This was paid to either the composer or the publishing company. BMI and ASCAP monitored the airwaves, set the royalty rates based on the media and the market size, and collected the revenue.

We formed our own publishing company, Opporknockity Music (from the old saying that "opporknockity only tunes once") and placed all our music in this entity with copyright protection. We agreed that we would only sign a contract if two key provisions were included. First, we would split the publishing with the record label 50/50. Established artists, those with a "track record," usually did at least this well, if not better. Secondly, we wanted to maintain artistic control. This was extremely important to us. We had met many artists who relinquished control to the producer and were unhappy with the final result.

Insisting on these two provisions proved to be our downfall. Negotiations at Fantasy reached a standstill in 1972, although we were still talking. Then Ralph's health took a turn for the worse and the discussions kind of fizzled out. Ralph left Fantasy and with him our key to the practice room.

Our efforts in the Fantasy practice rooms paid off. We now had the 50-60 songs we needed to play an entire night. This opened up many venues. Our strategy now was to play gigs locally so that we could save up enough to finance a trip to Hollywood and pitch ourselves to the record companies down south. We were usually able to get a gig in L.A. that would help us with travel expenses.

Armed with our Fantasy Records demos and some older tapes, Ron was able to get us more bookings. Jason's Shingle was a steak and lobster dinner house on Ski Run Boulevard, the main road to Heavenly Ski Resort in South Lake Tahoe, California. We were first booked there in late autumn or early winter of 1971. We played there four or five days running and it went very well. We were invited back and played there several times in the winter of 1971-1972 and throughout the next year or so.

We were booked for the last week of December 1971, which included New Year's Eve. Our pay included a place to stay. Jason's Shingle's owner had made arrangements for us to use a large suite at a nearby motel.

It had been snowing heavily for a couple days—really coming down, about an inch an hour. Steve had been out during the day and came across three young ladies who wanted to stay for New Year's Eve that night but had run out of money for a hotel. He had his eye on the blond. "If you want to stay, we have room at our place. It's not great, but you're welcome to stay and it's out of the snow."

"You have room for all of us?"

"Oh yeah. We can make it work. We're playing tonight…"

"What? What are you playing?"

"I'm in a band and we're playing at Jason's Shingle on Ski Run. You three can come in as our guests."

"Can we get in? We're all under 21."

"No problem. It's a dinner place. They serve food so it's OK to come in even if you're underage."

"OK. Where is it? We'll meet you there tonight." And they went off for the rest of the day.

That night, all three showed up. Besides the blond that Steve liked, there was a strawberry blond and an exotic looking brunette, who caught my eye. The place was really packed, the central fireplace was pouring out heat and a blizzard was sitting over the Tahoe Basin. We were having a wonderful New Year's Eve. After our last set, I was talking to a guy I'd met and he told me about this great party that was happening—lots of women. I wanted to go, hoping I would get lucky. I borrowed Scott's VW Bug and we headed for the party after a quick stop to pick up a bottle of tequila. The party was a bust. After we finished the bottle I went back to the motel, where I found my bed occupied. As I mentioned before, I was rather proprietary about my bed.

It was 3:00 AM. I was drunk and tired. I sat down in a rocking chair and stared at the stranger in my bed, considering my options. I didn't want to sleep in the chair and I couldn't stay up any longer. Stripping down to my T-shirt and underwear, I made up my mind and shook her awake. The brunette from the bar was fast asleep. "Hey, wake up." I shook her a little more and repeated myself. "Wake up!"

"Huh?" she opened her eyes and looked at me, finally coming to and looking a bit scared.

"You're in my bed. I need to get some sleep. Can you move over and let me in? I promise I won't touch you." That was an obvious lie, since it was a twin bed. "Please, I need some sleep." She scooted over and as I climbed in I noted that she was completely dressed including hat, jacket, muffler, and gloves. Then I reacted. Shaking her awake again I told her, "I don't mind you sleeping in my bed, but you have to take off your boots."

And that's how I met Debbie, the girl that I would eventually marry.[*]

---

[*] We were married in 1977 and are still happily together.

Chapter 8: Steak and Lobster

Spectrum Seekers find your way
Many try, but fall...

—*Spectrum Seekers, Scott Liggett*

I knew 1972 was going to be a great year. I had a new girlfriend and my hair had grown down to my shoulders. Bookings were becoming more regular and our audience was growing. We were going to sign some contracts for management and production of "Ravel" and it looked like we were making some inroads towards a record label.

There were a lot of dinner houses at Lake Tahoe and Sacramento that had a barnwood theme. These establishments paneled the walls with weathered wood from old barns that had been torn down. The menus centered on fondue, steak and lobster, and cocktails. Most of these were not large, with small stages at the front and seating 100-150 patrons in the bar/dining room. They really liked hiring us because we had no drums so we weren't overwhelming and we were a good draw for the venue. The Underground Shingle and Elegant Barn in Sacramento, Jason's Shingle at South Lake Tahoe, Generosity and Mother Lode in San Francisco, and Yank's Station in Meyers (Lake Tahoe), among others, were providing us a semi-regular but miniscule income.

I don't recall how we met Neil and Sandra Boorstyn. They had moved to the San Francisco Bay Area from New York to buy a bank. Neil was a heavy hitter in entertainment, specializing in intellectual property and copyright law. They were obviously very wealthy because not many have the wherewithal to buy a bank. They were interested in "Ravel," and so invited Steve and me to join them for breakfast at their house on Belvedere Island to discuss prospects. Steve and I parked on the street and stared at the house. It was not particularly large, but the entrance was a deck or bridge crossing the San Francisco Bay shoreline. There was a large opening in the middle where we looked down to see waves crashing against the rocks below. The house itself (with attached dock) was sitting on piers completely over the water. Sandra, who told us there was another guest coming, warmly greeted us at the door and invited us in. The furnishings were rather simple but the view was incredible. Sausalito, seeming close enough to touch, was directly across the water. Fisherman's Wharf in San Francisco was to the southwest, also unobstructed. Of course, we commented on the house and Sandra told us that they had waited a long time for a home to become available on West Shore Road so they were very happy to have found one they liked.[*]

The doorbell rang. Neil answered it and escorted in his guest. "Steve, David, I'd like you to meet David LaFlamme."

---

[*] In 2015, houses on this street range in price from $7.5M to $15.5M.

57

We shook his hand, "Pleased to meet you," we both mumbled. This was the first big star we had ever met in an intimate environment, not just at a gig.

"I really like your band," I told him. His eponymous album, "It's a Beautiful Day," had reached #47 on the U.S. charts in 1969. The band continued touring, performing a live KSAN-FM broadcast in 1971 and was one of the last acts to appear at Fillmore West in 1971.

"Sorry, Linda couldn't make it today," he told Neil, referring to his wife and keyboardist, who was also the lead vocalist on their biggest hit, "White Bird."

"That's too bad. Come on in, and we'll have a bite to eat."

We sat at the table and Steve and I looked at the spread. "What is this?" Steve asked, referring to the pink meat and round bread. I was just as perplexed, never having seen anything like it.

Neil laughed. "Lox and bagels. It's traditional." He proceeded to demonstrate by smearing on the cream cheese, adding capers, onions and lox. Sandra poured coffee.

"Wow. This is really good. I've never had this before," I told them. Steve would have agreed, but his mouth was full. I don't remember how much we ate, but I'm sure it was a lot.

We talked about the music business and filled Neil in on what we had been doing. After David LaFlamme left, we discussed "Ravel" and what we wanted to do with it. He thought there was a good chance that he could place it and offered to represent us to the Robert Stigwood Organization and others.

Upon returning to Stockton, we met with the other guys. "Wow. You should see this guy's place. It's amazing," Steve stated.

I chimed in, "Yea, it's even got it's own dock...but no boat."

"Well what happened?" asked Scott.

"We had lox and bagels. You know what that is?" I replied.

"Yea, I know," said Grode. "But what did he say?"

"This guy is some heavy hitter. He thinks he can place "Ravel" with Robert Stigwood. Of course, we will need to sign an agreement," answered Steve.

"I don't know..." from David K. "I don't want anyone messin' with the music."

"Who is this guy?" asked Scott.

"An attorney," said Steve. "He specializes in copyright and royalty law. His company's name is Royalty Control Corp."

"He'll probably try to rip us off," said David K.

"No he can't," I said. "Everything is already copyrighted. We'd have to sign off on it."

"Who is this guy?" asked Scott again.

"He has a lot of contacts. David LaFlamme was at his house with us," I said.

Steve chimed in, "He wants to place us with Robert Stigwood Organization. You know, RSO produced Cream and the Bee Gees."

"And 'Jesus Christ Superstar,' 'Hair,' and 'Grease,' " I added. "It could be the big time for us. We need to sign a contract."

"I don't know about that," said David K. with a nervous laugh. "We need complete artistic control. I don't want to get ripped off." David K. was very apprehensive about making commitments.

"He wants to represent us?" asked Grode. "For how long? What's in it for him?"

"Here's his contract," offered Steve, passing out a couple copies.

"This looks really good," said Grode. "We need to move on it."

We finally agreed that we should sign, so the next day we all trekked back to San Francisco to Neil's office in the Embarcadero Center and signed a deal on January 10, 1972 for 6-month exclusive placement rights to "Ravel." Upon successful placement he would receive 15% of royalties.

It seemed we were in a contract-signing mood. Ron Cornelius was a well-known musician living in San Francisco. He had a band called West in the late 1960's that had broken up, subsequently freeing him to do studio work in Nashville for artists who were being produced by Bob Johnston, an up-and-coming producer for Columbia Records. Ron worked on albums with Johnny Cash, Bob Dylan, Flatt & Scruggs, Simon and Garfunkle, and Leonard Cohen. He appeared on many of Bob Dylan's albums and later played lead guitar for Leonard Cohen on world tours.

He had been approached by Polydor to produce a solo album, which he titled "Tin Luck." His contract with Polydor included a provision that he would do the self-produced album only if they allowed him to produce a couple other acts that he selected. He must have seen us around the Bay Area because he was interested in working with us. About the same time as the deal with Royalty Control Corp. was coming together, he proposed that we sign a 90-day exclusive contract with him. We armed him with demo tapes. He wanted to place us with Polydor or any other interested party. The contract with him had no terms, but we agreed that, if something happened, we would make it worth his while. He was OK with that and we were very pleased to have a handshake deal. We checked with Neil and he said it was OK with him so long as "Ravel" was not included, so we signed that contract too (January 11, 1972).

I was so happy that things were on the upswing that I wrote a letter to my new girlfriend, Debbie, to tell her how close I was to becoming a big rock 'n' roll star. [*] I sent her a token of my love—a stick of musk incense, which I explained was made from the genitals of a buck deer. I asked for her birth information so I could prepare her astrological chart, which I thought might be a pathway

---

[*] This was the start of a lengthy correspondence between us that lasted until the last days of the band. I found these letters recently and they are a great reference for key events until the band disintegrated in 1974.

into her pants. I had previously had some success with this technique, so I was hopeful. She sent me her "Certificate of Live Birth." I did her chart but the payoff didn't happen until many months had passed.

Chapter 9: Four Cents and a Stamp

Well there ain't much more that one man can do to change,
I've got those sit down, worn out, 14-mile workday blues

—*Poverty Song, Steve Solari*

After leaving Jason's Shingle, we went to Santa Cruz and played at some place that Ron Cornelius had arranged. We had a great time hanging with Ron, listening to tapes of his old band, and trying to figure out how to get us ahead. Polydor was not interested, but Ron said that he was working on EMI to possibly record us in John Lennon's studio in London. He was also talking to ABC-Paramount, discussing the possibility of recording in Bob Dylan's studio in Nashville, where Ron Cornelius worked with him. "In any case," I wrote to Debbie, "we'll be in Nashville on April 25, 1972 to put on 'Ravel' in an old castle,[*] surrounded by cherry blossoms." Of course, none of this happened.

I was incredibly broke and in a rotten mood. In my letters to Debbie I blamed Stuart Little for my ongoing poverty. Still, I loved the music and the life of an itinerant musician. I had to get some extra income.

---

[*] I believe this was the Castle Gwynn when it was just starting to be a music venue.

I hit upon an idea. In order to copyright our songs we had to send in lead sheets to the copyright office. A lead sheet is the chords, melody and lyrics all written together. I had written all the lead sheets for our material and I thought there might be a niche for my work elsewhere. I asked Neil and he put me in touch with Taj Mahal. I received a couple of tapes and wrote out the lead sheets, for which I received $15.00 each. That was great. If I made $15.00 on a gig (after expenses) it was pretty good. Even better, I could do this during downtime, of which there was plenty.

In January 1972 we returned to Jason's. This was always welcome because the club provided us with a place to stay, regular meals, and a little income. I wrote Debbie that when we arrived I had four cents in my pocket, one or two sheets of paper and a couple stamps. We usually stayed for a week or more. The meals provided by the dinner house were steak, fondue, and salad. We weren't allowed free lobster. The diet was pretty boring and I was gaining weight, contributing to my unhappiness.

Between gigs in February we returned to the Central Valley. David K. had moved up to Mokelumne Hill where Scott still lived. I was staying in Stockton with the girl I met when I moved out of Grode's playhouse. Our next gigs were in Sacramento at the Elegant Barn and the Underground Shingle. Our gig at the Elegant Barn was frustrating because it was just a pickup joint and there weren't more than a handful of people actually listening to us. The Underground Shingle was better because we were appreciated even though we were no closer to a record deal. At least we were working and solidifying a circuit of dinner houses where we could earn a little income. We were very successful in maintaining this "Steak & Lobster" circuit because without drums we weren't loud, and we could easily fit on a small stage. These dinner houses became our bread and butter for the next couple years.

"I have more good news," I wrote on February 23, 1972. "We have some people coming to hear 'Ravel' in a couple of weeks. They're with Bell Records. They have a show open in New York and L.A. called 'Godspell' and they might be interested in putting up the money to open 'Ravel' on Broadway in New York. It'll cost about a half million. That's a lot of money." We had also been talking to the Robert Stigwood Organization (through Neil Boorstyn). RSO had four or five ongoing shows of "Jesus Christ Superstar" with scheduled openings for two more and five touring companies. "We'll also probably be up in Washington doing concerts for crowds of 8,000-10,000 people earning over $250 per week after expenses," I wrote. "I could even pay back the $400 I owe my parents." There was also talk about a show with Ike and Tina Turner at the Circle Star Theater in San Carlos, CA. The talks with RSO continued but nothing else materialized. Bell Records, Columbia, and Warner Brothers were topics of speculation, but no more than that.

We played a benefit for Zero Population Growth in the Bay Area. The kids and parents loved us. "Big deal. We were still broke," I wrote, " and not any closer to a recording studio…than when we met…It's a cruel world." This was a busy week. We were booked at Sproul Plaza at U.C. Berkeley, New Orleans House two nights, St. Mary's College in Moraga, and Stanford in Palo Alto. Altogether it was five gigs in three days and then back to Lake Tahoe.

We loved playing at Jason's Shingle. The crowd was receptive and management really treated us well. Grode was still with us full time. He was becoming increasingly moody and I was becoming increasingly insensitive to him. However, our disagreements resolved quickly and didn't interfere with the unity of the band. We depended on each other's support because we were all working for success.

It continued snowing heavily that season at Lake Tahoe. We attracted a lot of locals to Jason's Shingle, which the owner appreciated because he was not totally dependent on the tourists who had come to ski.

"How would you like to come skiing with us?" a couple local ladies asked me at the end of an evening performance.

"It sounds really good, but I've never done it before."

"It's easy. We'll show you how."

I had a ski parka, knit hat, and some really thin gloves, so I asked Ron Schwartz what else I needed. He was a very experienced skier. He handed me a pair of gaiters and suggested that I get a can of Scotchguard and waterproof my jeans. I knew some guys at a ski rental shop, so they set me up with free gear.

The girls picked me up and we headed up to Donner Ski Ranch, a small family resort west of South Lake Tahoe. Arriving there, I put on my gear and they showed me how to get on the lift. I promptly fell on my butt getting off at the top of the bunny hill.

They got me pointed down the hill and told me, "Put your skis like this," making a wedge with the tips close and tails apart. "This is called a snowplow. You turn by putting weight on one ski or the other." One of them demonstrated and had me follow. After about 15-20 feet I crossed my tips and fell on my face. We worked our way down the slope with them helping me up every few yards when I fell. We took another ride up the lift and they took one more laborious trip with me down the bunny hill.

"You've got it now. We'll see you later," and they took off for parts unknown.

I kept riding the lift and falling all over the place on my way down and then doing it again. I stared enviously at the little kids zooming past me and tried to figure out what they were doing that I wasn't. By the end of the day when the ladies came back to get me I was soaking wet, frozen solid, and covered with ice and snow from head to foot. I looked like the Abominable Snowman, but I had actually made a few successful turns and discovered a wonderful feeling of freedom. As crummy as I was, there were moments when I envisioned what could be. Those women gave me one of the greatest gifts I have ever received; my first day on skis.

Unfortunately I couldn't afford to continue the sport at that time but I hoped that some day I would be able to. I still ski today as much as I can. I have never lost the thrill of going downhill that I experienced that day. I wish I could thank those two women.

Winter turned to Spring. We had gigs at the Mother Lode and North Beach Revival (Carol Doda's Club) in San Francisco, and senior proms at some Sacramento high schools. Things were kind of slowing down.

Grode was always looking for something out of the mainstream and somehow he came across a group in Los Angeles that was experimenting with Chroma key (now called greenscreen). They offered to make a video of us at no charge so they could demonstrate the technology. So in the summer of 1972 we packed our robes and a recording of Grode's song, "Burn the Wind," and drove down to L.A. to make the video. Bernie came with us and was the featured performer doing mime during the song.

The video recording session was a cattle call. We waited for our turn, following Loggins and Messina, David Bowie, Billy Paul and others. When it was our turn we donned our robes and went on the stage, waited for some lighting adjustments, and lip-synced "Burn the Wind." The guitars weren't even plugged in and we had no drummer although there was a drum part on the tape. I didn't play on the recording, so I put on a robe and synced the drum parts. It was very easy. I just had to be sure to time the cymbal crashes correctly. The video turned out very good—lots of light-show effects, close-ups of Bernie, pans across the band with solarization and a great sounding recording.

In the fall of 1972 we had a big show at UOP. We were the warm-up act for the Sons of Champlin. Then our tape of "Burn the Wind" was aired on national television on "Superstars of Rock," hosted by Wolfman Jack. We had to join AFTRA (American Federation of Television and Radio Actors) and pay $25.00 initiation fee. We eventually each received a royalty check for $93.00 from SRO Productions. What an easy way to get money! I took my newfound wealth and rushed out to buy a pair of Earth Shoes sandals—very hippie.

1972 ended in the Santa Cruz Mountains at a Hell's Angels club called The Chateau. We were apprehensive about playing there, especially since there had been a stabbing there the night before, but we needed the pay. It was a very rough crowd but surprisingly they liked us and danced.

Chapter 10: Where'd Everybody Go?

I won't pretend that I do not miss you
I won't pretend I don't call your name

—The Light That Shines in Your Eyes, Steve Solari

"That guy's a crook. I've never trusted him," Neil Boorstyn informed us when we told him that Rik Gunnel had shown interest in producing us. "You guys stay away from him."

We were meeting with Neil in San Francisco before we left to go play at the Troubador[*] in West Hollywood, where we were scheduled to warm up for Bette Midler, who was promoting her first album, "The Divine Miss M." released in November 1972.

A guy named Eddie Choran wanted to manage us. He worked for Rik Gunnel, who had sold his nightclub and management company in England to Robert Stigwood, then became the Robert Stigwood Organization representative in the U.S. Eddie was the guy who got us booked into the Troubador.

At the club, we did our sound check in the afternoon then returned to our rooms for a little rest and to review our set list and pump each other up. We were so antsy. This was the most important gig we had ever played. We even had some of our fans coming from Stockton to see us.

---

[*] The Troubador opened in 1957. It remains one of the major venues in L.A. Numerous top artists have performed and recorded there.

Before the show I met up with a couple guys who had made the trip from Stockton to L.A. We went for dinner then headed over to the nightclub. One of my friends asked me to check the ticket price when they dropped me off in front. When I told them how much, their faces dropped. "That's a lot. We don't have that much money. Maybe we can panhandle to pick up a few more bucks."

"No way," I replied, "look what I found." When I had walked up to the ticket window I noticed something on the sidewalk. It was a folded up $10 bill. I gave them the money for their tickets. I was pretty happy. This was a particularly good omen.

Showtime: We were assembled on stage, all tuned up, set lists at our feet and ready to go. The spotlight came on and the emcee announced, "Ladies and Gentlemen, the Troubador proudly presents The Stuart Little Band." Then the stage lights came up, we looked at each other for the count then David K. immediately took off his guitar and set it down. "What are you doing?" Grode asked him.

"I have to take a leak."

"What the…" from Steve. "Can't it wait?"

"No. I have to go now," and he left the stage, leaving us sitting on our stools like a bunch of yahoos.

"We're from Stockton," announced Steve, trying to fill the time.

71

"We're from a farm in the Central Valley," I added. Grode played a couple small riffs on harmonica.

"We're sorry to keep you waiting," from Scott, "but our guitarist had to step away for a minute."

From me, "He had to answer a call of nature." It was not long but seemed forever before he returned. He came back to a round of applause and, as usual, just chuckling quietly to himself, picked up his guitar and nodded his head. We were ready.

"OK. Here we go," announced Steve and we launched into our opening song. The set was very successful and we received many favorable comments from people afterwards, including Doug Weston, the owner of the club. This was definitely the big time.

Eddie had brought Rik Gunnel to the show. Backstage after our set we were introduced. "I like you guys," Rik told us. "I think we can do something together."

We talked a little bit, filled him in on our history and told him about "Ravel."

"I have to go somewhere tonight, but I'd like to get together with you. Can you come to the Rainbow Bar and Grill tomorrow night? You can be my guests upstairs at Over the Rainbow."

"Don't miss this," Eddie told us after Rik left. "This is a very exclusive club. You only get in if you're invited. And you gotta talk to Rik. He can make things happen."

We showed up the next night. The place was dimly lit and packed. I knew there were famous people there but I was too busy eating and drinking to notice. Scott, maybe not as hampered by drink as I was, noticed John Lennon sitting in a corner looking very morose. Then later, after a few more cocktails, Scott turned around and bumped into somebody. "Hey...aren't you Elton John?" he slurred. The reply was affirmative so Scott answered, "Well...I'm Scotty Liggett," as if he was SOMEBODY.

"Hey Ron," I asked Ron Schwartz. Where'd you get the big cigar?

"At the bar. Want one?"

"I don't know, they're probably pretty expensive," I answered naively.

"Don't worry, we're on Rik's tab." So I made my selection. This was my first experience with someone else's expense account. So we smoked, and drank, and ate, and drank some more.

"Bartender, put this on Rik Gunnel's tab," we said over and over until we were all totally plastered and stuffed with gourmet food. We were on top of the world, happy as pigs in shit.

We thanked Rik for a great night. He gave us his address and told us to come up to his house in the Hollywood Hills the next afternoon.

We found his house, which was a huge mansion that had once belonged to one of the Keystone Kops. There was a gigantic iron double gate between two stone pillars leading into a circular drive surrounding a fountain. We parked the Green Hornet near the Mercedes and BMW luxury sedans that were already there, then mounted the wide marble steps and passed between stone columns leading to the nine-foot tall double door entrance.

"Can you believe this?" I asked the guys.

"Wow. We've really hit the jackpot," said Grode.

Ron walked right up to the door, lifted the doorknocker and banged it a couple times. A very good-looking young lady opened the door. "Yes? Can I help you?"

"We're here to see Rik. He asked us to come by today."

"Oh, are you the Stuart Little Band? Please come in. He's expecting you." We entered the very large but sparsely furnished living room. "Have a seat and I'll get Rik," then she walked out.

Rik came down looking considerably more refreshed than we felt. With the exception of Grode, we were all feeling the effects of the night before. Rik sat down with us and we started talking business. We talked about royalties and publishing income, tour and recording expenses, distribution problems, where we could possibly record, etc. He didn't make any commitments but to our relief he understood that we wanted to keep some of the money that we could potentially make. He didn't shoot us down for this in spite of our not having a track record. "I'll get something drawn up and sent to you," he told us in parting. "You should get it in about a week or two."

We made our way back to Stockton and waited. He called us a couple weeks later to tell us that he was sending something in the mail for us to look at.

Back in San Francisco, we met again with Neil Boorstyn to fill him in on what had been going on. We told him we had signed a management agreement with Eddie Choran Enterprises assuring Neil that he still had exclusive rights to "Ravel.

"That's fine," he replied. "But what's Eddie Choran going to do for you?"

"He got us a recording contract offer from Rik Gunnel for RSO Records."

"I told you guys not to do that. Believe me, you're making a big mistake."

Naturally, we didn't believe him.

"I'm warning you. Stay away from him. He's not a good guy."

"Are you pissed off at us?" we asked. "This looks like we could be finally producing a record. It's a great opportunity and nothing else is happening."

"Just be patient, "he told us. "These things take time. So what are your plans now?" he asked.

"I think we need to go with Eddie and Rik. It looks like it could really be happening for us."

"Well, you forced me into this. I hate to do it, but I'm going to have to cut you loose."

"What? Why? Come on Neil," we begged him. "We're counting on you."

"Sorry guys, but you're not following my advice so I can't help you anymore."

"But…but…" we were flabbergasted. "We're counting on you…"

"Sorry guys, it's not personal, just business. I wish you luck."

"Well, thanks for all your help." We shook hands and filed out of his office.

We received the contract from Rik. It wasn't what we wanted, but it was something. We called him back and said we'd like to meet to discuss a couple points. We made an appointment and then drove back to L.A. to meet with him. The meeting went well and he agreed to some of our changes. "I'll get this re-written and sent back to you guys. Expect it in a couple days."

Sure enough, the document arrived at the Solari Farm and it looked pretty good except we wanted to see if we could get a few more concessions. We were willing to sign it as it was, even though it was less than we had hoped for. We called Rik and made another appointment for the next week.

We were pumped up on the drive up to his house. This was it—the Big Break. We were on the road to stardom. Or so it seemed until we got up to his house. The double gate was swinging half open, the fountain was not running and there was only a small economy car in the driveway. We parked and walked up to the front doors, which were also halfway open and swinging in the wind. We entered and stared in amazement. The place was empty except for a couple chairs and some random papers blowing around the room. It was deathly quiet. We noticed the young lady who had greeted us previously was sitting in a dark corner with her head in her hands. "What happened here?" we asked. "Where is everybody?" She was practically in tears. "I don't know. I came up here and it was just like this. I guess I'll have to get a job now," and she put her head back in her hands. She couldn't tell us a thing about what happened except that everybody was there yesterday and now they're gone.*

We made our way back to Stockton. We agreed that we should meet with Neil to see if there was a chance he would take us back, so Steve and I went to his office at the Embarcadero Center in San Francisco and told him what happened. "I told you guys that he was bad news," he stated. "I heard there were people looking for him. Like I said, I wish you luck. Sorry I can't help you anymore."

---

* I discovered many years later that Rik had become disgusted with the entertainment business and disappeared for six years, traveling incognito in Australia and Viet Nam. He resurfaced in the Austrian ski resort of Kitzbühl where he opened a small bar and later a larger venue called the Londoner, which he ran until his death in 2007 at age 75.

Stuart Little Band at UOP Stadium, Byrds conceert 1968
L-R: Stephen Solari, David Hoiem, Perry Karraker, Phil McKay, David Kemp

Perry Karraker, 1970

David Kemp, 1970

Bernie Bang, 1969

Loading the white pickup, 1970

Steve Solari 1969

Gordon Clark, 1970

Phil McKay 1970

Handbills, 1971 and 1972

David Hoiem 1970

Lake Tahoe, 1972
Grode, David H., Steve,
Scott, David K

Steve, David H.,
Grode, Scott, David K.

Sacramento, 1973
Steve, Scott,Grode, David K.
David H.

Publicity photo, 1974

Chapter 11: Selling Soap

It's all right to have a dream
But just don't make believe it's real

—*What Do You Have, Phil McKay*

"I don't know how much to charge. We've never rented a room for that long before," replied the young lady at the front desk of the sleaziest motel we could find in Calabasas.

"How long do you usually rent a room for?" I asked.

"Usually just an hour or two. Sheets are extra."

We had requested two rooms for two nights. We had never heard of hourly motels, so we went in search of a slightly less seedy motel.

This was in October 1972 when we got booked to play at a roadside inn during the Calabasas Pumpkin Festival. We were lucky to get the gig. It was a new venue for us and we desperately needed the gig to finance this particular trip to L.A. Ron Schwartz had somehow finagled an appointment with the President of Capitol Records, Alan Livingston. His office was located at the top of the famous building that resembles a stack of LP records, adjacent to Hollywood and Vine. This was the most important person we had yet met and we were nervous as hell.

We entered the lobby, found the elevators and got in. "OK guys, this is the big time finally," said Steve.

"No kidding," agreed Scott. "We need to play it real cool."

"Hey David," I said. "Just be real quiet and let Steve and Ron do most of the talking," I suggested.

"OK," he answered. "I wouldn't know what to say anyway. Make sure he doesn't want to prostitute the music."

We stepped off the elevator into the plush reception area.

"Please have a seat. I'll see if he's ready for you," greeted the overly made-up young lady seated at the desk. "Would you like some refreshments?"

"Oh no, we're fine," and we sat down and fidgeted. After what seemed hours but was really not long at all, we were ushered into a very large office. On the credenza behind the desk were a couple tape players. Scattered around the office were hundreds of reel-to-reel and cassette tapes, LP's, and other rock paraphernalia covering every available flat surface. Framed posters and t-shirts were hanging on the walls.

"Howdy guys. How ya' doin' today?" Alan greeted us. "Have a seat."

We mumbled our greetings, introduced ourselves and thanked him for meeting with us.

"I liked what you sent me. Let's have a listen." He turned around and started his tape player, which amazingly enough, had our latest demo tape already cued up and ready to play. We sat and listened while we told him about "Ravel" and the fact that we had lots of other material and were constantly writing new stuff.

"Our studios are booked up but there's a new studio openin' up down here. It's called Sound City. I'm gonna get you some demo time there. I'd like to see more of what you can do."

"Thank you," said Steve. "When do you want us there?"

After calling the studio, he told us, "11:00 tomorrow morning. You'll have six hours. How many songs can you get done?"

We told him we could get one or maybe two in that time.

"Great. Come back on Thursday (the day after the recording) and we'll see what you've got."

Sound City Studios was so new it was still under construction. They had one brand-new, state-of-the-art studio completed. The mixing board was the largest we had ever seen, maybe fifteen or twenty feet long. We were very impressed but under a horrific time constraint, so after a quick tour including their uncompleted live echo chamber (a small cement room with no wall parallel to another wall) we entered the studio and set up. Since we had no drums, setup and sound check was considerably quicker than it would have been for other bands. I don't remember what we recorded, but I think we got two songs into a rough mix.

The next day, back at Capitol Records, feeling much more confident, we entered the same office and played our new tape.

"I like it, but you need drums," he told us.

"Well, we haven't been able to find a drummer that we like yet."

"We can fix that," he told us. "But the main thing I want to know is, what can you do for me?"

Ron answered, "We can sell a lot of records."

We then mentioned that we already had a publishing company, Opporknockity Music. We told him that we would like to keep some of the publishing and royalty monies for ourselves and maintain artistic control. As we went on, he sat up a little straighter and looked at us somewhat bemused. "You may want to rethink what ya want. Tell me, what's so special about you guys? You're not offering anything new or different. I could be selling soap."

We left the building saying to ourselves that this was another case of, "don't call us, we'll call you." Which is exactly how it turned out. The only thing we got from our meeting was an addition to our growing library of demo tapes.

We went back to the Bay Area where we had a few gigs lined up in addition to our regular steak-and-lobster circuit.

We played at a couple high school proms and put on an upscaled performance of "Ravel" at St. Mary's High School. It was our first staging using a dancer in addition to our usual complement of the band plus Bernie. We also took this performance to an American Cancer Society benefit at the Fresno Convention Center and then to L.A. for a couple smaller shows.

Returning to Northern California, we played at the Town and Country Lodge in Santa Cruz, opening for Charles Lloyd, who was one of my idols from my high school days. He was a great disappointment. He was so drunk he could hardly play. I was very disappointed and quickly tired of listening to him so I made my way to the rear exit to go outside for some fresh air. Standing near the door was an older black lady escorted by two younger black guys. "Hello," I said. "You look like somebody important."

She gave me a big smile. "I'm Big Mama Thornton."

"Oh my God! I'm so pleased to meet you. I've read a lot about you."

"See," she said as she turned to her escorts. "He knows who I am."

We chatted for a while about the vagaries of the music business and then she told me she had to leave and stepped out the back door.

Before Spring Break of 1973 we were booked at Cal Poly San Luis Obispo. The main act was Cold Blood. It turned out to be quite an eventful evening. It started out normally, we waited for Cold Blood to finish their sound check then we went up for ours. Everything was going fine until Scott touched one of the microphones with his lips. There was a tremendous blue electric arc and Scott was thrown back about eight feet, landing on top of the drum set. He was kind of out of it and had a huge blister on his lip, but eventually recovered enough to finish the sound check. Needless to say, we did not get close to the microphones and were apprehensive about doing the show, even though the stage manager assured us that the short had been fixed.

When it was time for our set we walked out on stage, the guys plugged in and we started the first few bars of our opener when, WHANG!!! Steve stopped playing. There went our rhythm so we all stopped.

"Hey guys. I broke a string."

"What? You gotta be kidding. Nobody breaks a bass string."

"Well I did."

"Where the hell can we get a bass string at 10:00 PM on a Saturday night?" we were all thinking. It wouldn't do to have Steve borrow another bass. He played an Ovation fretless bass, which had a very punchy sound and was the beat we all followed. A fretted bass would be too smooth and would emphasize our lack of drums.

A friend of Scott's, Dave Frank, who was standing on the side of the stage, saw what happened and jumped in to help. "Steve, what string is that?"

"It's my G-string."

Dave walked up to the mike. "Does anybody have a G-string?" Laughter arose from the audience. "No, I'm serious. The bass player broke his G-string and the band can't play without a bass. We need a bass guitar G-string so we can do our set and bring on Cold Blood."

As luck would have it, there was a guy in the audience that owned a music store that was fortunately not far away. He came up to the stage and told us he'd get one for us as soon as he could. We left the stage. In about 15-20 minutes he returned, Steve repaired the bass and we played a good set. Once again, we got comments from people that didn't even notice that we were without drums.

Chapter 12: The Idle Poor

Suddenly it seems that that's not all
It seems that tomorrow's waiting in the hall

—Sigma Phi Nothing, Phil McKay

"Another dreary, gray, rainy day in the flatlands," I wrote to Debbie in mid-January 1973. Winter in the Central Valley is very depressing. It is always cold, damp, and oftentimes smoggy because of an inversion layer. The sky is constantly overcast with dim sunlight barely filtering through the clouds. The sun is often hidden for two or three weeks at a stretch. Every day is gray and gloomy. "I'll sure be glad when I can afford to live somewhere (anywhere) else," I wrote.

After our success at the Troubador we expected to get The Big Break we had been waiting for. There were feelers from Warner Bros. and RCA and of course, RSO was talking to us. But we had yet to see anything in writing.

Eddie had a lot of contacts in addition to RSO. He set up an audition with Suzanne de Passe, who was the Vice President of Motown and assistant to Barry Gordy, Motown's President and founder. This led to talks with Motown. He also had connections at

Polydor, where we had failed to make progress with Ron Cornelius, but Eddie was able to get us in and began talks there, too.

We took another trip to L.A. and stayed with Brian Williams, a friend of Eddie's, at a big multi-level fixer-upper house on Appian Way, built on stilts cantilevered over the seismically unstable hillside above Hollywood. The house was huge with incredible views but in desperate need of repair and additional furniture. Still it was a roof and a place to sleep while we pushed our music in La-La Land. Our host, Brian, was a practicing Nicheren Shoshu Buddhist and asked if we wanted to join him in the evening prayer session at the temple. I was curious, so I went along with him and Hilton Valentine (the guitarist for The Animals). The room was dimly lit, filled with incense and lots of people, mostly, if not all male, on their knees chanting, "Nam-Myoho-Renge-Kyo," while they rubbed a string of wooden beads in their hands with a repetitive clicking sound. It was mesmerizing and induced a kind of trance in me. I was transfixed.

"Brian, I asked, "what is the chant for?

"We believe that the chant channels energy into your visions and dreams. All you have to do to make your dreams come true is keep chanting and they will be realized."

Well, it sounded like a good idea, especially since my

dreams were continually being dashed on the rocks. "How can I join?"

"You really want to?"

"Yes."

"You can join tonight. It's a very small ceremony and we will give you a set of beads."

"OK. Let's do it."

So that night I became a Buddhist, based on the very un-Buddhist hope of securing wealth and fame, rather than discovering the path to enlightenment.

The next morning I awoke and went into the kitchen and met up with Hilton who was having his morning "Health Cocktail" which consisted of filling two juice glasses: one with vitamins and supplements and the other with white wine, then alternating between the two until they were both empty. We chanted a bit and then Brian, Hilton, and the band made our way to Paramount Studios, where we were recording some demos for RSO. Hilton joined us on a couple of songs. They came out really nice, especially "Sunset Sunrise" with Hilton playing bongos.

A week later, on February 22,1973 we signed a management contract with Eddie Choran. It was for one year with three one-year options. We were still waiting for an answer from Polydor and Motown.

After the disappearance of Rik Gunnel, Eddie had been promoted to director at RSO. We thought that maybe, just maybe this time, we would get a recording contract signed. Eddie had great connections and was very enthusiastic about Stuart Little. We just had to be patient and it would all eventually work out.

Back in the Solari garage, Ron S. showed up at practice one day. We were still elated from the Troubador gig and the great demos we had just finished with Hilton. "Hey guys! You won't believe what I've got!" yelled Ron, as he came strutting in.

"Wait a minute. We're working on this song."

"Just forget it for a minute," said Ron. "This is really good."

"OK Ron. What's so great?"

"I've got us booked in Sun Valley, Idaho. For two weeks. With rooms, meals and lift passes."

We couldn't believe it. "C'mon Ron, quit bullshitting us."

"No, it's for real. We have to be there in two weeks."

"Are we getting paid?"

"Of course. We don't work for nothin'. You guys will have a great time."

I was so excited. First the Troubador and then this. "Maybe the Buddhist chanting worked," I thought to myself.

"Where are we staying?" we asked him.

"Right in the Village, in the center of everything. I'll teach you guys how to ski. You'll have a great experience and make some money, too." I couldn't believe our luck. Things were finally taking a turn for the better. I would learn to ski for free at a world-famous ski resort. And, on top of that get paid for being there.

We loaded up the VW Microbus and the Green Hornet and headed towards Reno. I was driving the van with Ron, and the rest of the guys were with Steve. Ron and I opted to drive non-stop because we didn't want to spend money for a motel. It is 715 miles from Stockton, California to Sun Valley, Idaho. We left on Saturday afternoon and took turns driving. Most of the route is in the high desert northeast of Reno until you turn north in Wells, NV. Shortly outside Reno it started snowing, getting progressively heavier as time went on. We slowed down a lot, following in the tracks of the big rigs. The snow was coming down and the wind rocked the van as the blizzard gained intensity. The crappy VW heater was barely keeping up. After leaving Wells, we passed through Jackpot, NV and entered Idaho with the sun starting to come up. A couple hours later we pulled into a Denny's in Twin Falls, Idaho for breakfast. It was Sunday morning and many families were dressed very nicely, having breakfast before heading off to church.

We walked in and immediately felt unwelcome. Here we were, a couple long-haired, bearded, smelly (we had been driving for over 13 hours non-stop) hippies coming out of a VW van with flowered curtains in the windows. The place went deathly quiet as everybody stared at the apparitions before them. We just wanted breakfast and coffee, so we tried to be inconspicuous, but it wasn't working. We eventually got seated at an out-of-the-way corner, but the stares and hostility did not stop. We got out of there as fast as we could and headed for the resort, another hour or two north.

Arriving at the Village, we immediately noticed that almost everybody there was obviously very wealthy and very much into being a part of the ski resort scene. It felt like a movie set with all the rich people wandering around dressed in furs and expensive ski outfits. We checked in with the resort, unloaded our gear and found our assigned room. The rest of the guys were arriving the next day and we were scheduled to play the following night. We were to play during après ski in the bar on Tuesday to Sunday for two weeks. Meals were provided in the employee dining room.

Ron and I walked around looking in the high-priced shops, eventually ending up in the ski rental shop where we started talking to the guys there. "Yea, we're booked here for two weeks. You should come and hear us."

"Where are you playing?

"Main lodge. We start tomorrow."

"What kind of music you guys play?"

This was always a hard question to answer, as our sound didn't fit neatly into any category. "It's all original, kind of folk-rock-jazz. You'd probably like it."

"We'll come by. What time you start?"

"Five o'clock. Every night but Monday."

"Cool. Say, did you guys bring your gear?"

"You mean ski gear?" I asked. "Yea. Ron did, I don't have any. I don't even know how to ski. I've only done it once and I fell a lot."

"That's how you learn. You guys come by tomorrow morning and we'll get you set up."

"How much will that cost?" I asked. "I can't afford a lot."

"No charge, courtesy of the house. Just don't tell anyone. Only for you guys and whoever else is with you."

"Wow, man. Thank you."

"Cool. Just see either one of us when you come in. Don't talk to anyone else in the shop."

The next morning we picked up our lift passes and went to the ski shop to get fitted. Ron took me up to Dollar Mountain, which is the beginner mountain adjacent to the Village. The big mountain is Bald Mountain, which is a short shuttle bus ride from the Village. Ron, being a certified instructor, was able to give me some valuable pointers and I fell less often. We broke off mid-afternoon and went into the Village to meet the other guys.

"When did you get here?" I asked Steve.

"We've been here for two hours. Where the hell have you been?"

"Up there," I pointed up the hill. "We get free ski gear."

"No kidding."

"Yea, let's go over to the ski shop and get you fitted so you can ski tomorrow. Ron helped me out a lot."

"I'll get you started, but I'm not going to hang out with you on the bunny hill all day," said Ron.

"Let's go," I said.

"Not me," said David K. "I don't want to ski." So Ron, Steve, Scott and I went to get ski gear and take it back to our rooms.

The next day we had breakfast and skied most of the day, using very short skis. At that time the newest learning method was GLM, Graduated Length Method. We started on short skis and as our skills improved we "graduated" to progressively longer skis. I skied every day, making it back to our gig just in time to go on stage, then got up early to go back on the hill the next day. We eventually moved over to Bald Mountain and, with longer skis and great difficulty, skied some steeper runs. We rode the first chairlift that was installed in North America, operational in winter 1937, a single chair on Exhibition on Bald Mountain.[*] It was really a bad snow year at Sun Valley so they hadn't groomed any of the slopes. Conditions were very difficult. Some of the moguls were as big as Volkswagens and solid ice. In any case, I was hooked for life.

We were well received and everything was going very well, practically a vacation just like wealthy people enjoy. I finally realized that the idle poor can sometimes have it just as good as the

---

[*] In 1974 this chairlift was purchased by the Sheridan Ski Club and re-installed on Mount Eyak in Alaska. It is the oldest working chairlift in North America. In addition to this lift they have a rope tow.

idle rich.

Right at the end, just before we left, Steve got sick. He played the last night or two and then went to the infirmary where he was diagnosed with pneumonia. The doctor said he was not used to treating this illness. He usually treated broken bones and other traumatic injuries. Steve had to stay a few days after we were done, so we all drove back without him. Ron and I again driving the VW van and everyone but Steve in the Green Hornet. Steve had to fly back from Ketchum. He said it cost him $1500 for the airfare and the hospital bill.

Steve barely made it back in time for the scheduled performance of "Ravel" with the entire dance troupe and Bernie. We were doing a premier stage performance at the UOP Conservatory Auditorium, a beautiful, intimate theater on the UOP campus. We had Bernie and the John Casserly Dancers, who had been rehearsing their parts with Grode while we were away in L.A. and Sun Valley. Once again, it was a sellout audience and everybody loved the show.

Ron S. had invited his cousin, Robert Blumenthal and his wife, Inez, to come to the "Ravel" performance. Bob was a temporarily retired marine salvage attorney. He had a lot of time on his hands because his accountant had told him he had made too much money and he needed to take a couple years off. They and their two children lived in Kentfield, a very exclusive community in Marin County. The large house was situated on a forested hillside and had a swimming pool .

Bob and Inez became interested in Stuart Little and decided that they wanted to be a part of the rock music scene so they "adopted" us. We often stayed at their house in Kentfield when we had gigs in the Bay Area. We ate meals with them, swam in their pool ,and just hung out at the house. What a welcome change from the gloom and fog in Stockton. In exchange, we did a few chores, discussed our trials and tribulations with them and invited them to our local gigs. We were playing at the Sweetwater in Mill Valley quite a bit and were starting to get some regular bookings at the Great American Music Hall in San Francisco, as well as other well-known venues around the Bay Area.

" We really like your music and you're a great bunch of guys. Is there anything we can do to help you out?" Bob and Inez asked us one afternoon.

"No, we appreciate everything you're doing for us now," said Steve. This was in August 1973. Bob had agreed to provide legal counsel for us for "Ravel," since we had lost representation from Neil Boorstyn. We signed a contract wherein Robert Blumenthal received 5% of gross revenues from "Ravel."

Although not part of the agreement, Bob wanted to help us further with some equipment upgrades. Our amplifiers and PA system were pretty basic, but they met our needs.

"What do you guys need?" he asked.

"There is something if it's not too much too ask," I inquired. Scott and I were playing some pretty funky instruments, so I figured the worst that could happen is that I would be told "no," which was not a new occurrence in my life. "I could really use a new flute. Mine is just a student model. I could sound a lot better with a better instrument. Could I get a loan for something new?"

"Me, too," Scott chimed in. I could use a better guitar."

"OK, you guys pick something out and let me know what you find, then we'll talk about it."

A few days later, Scott told him, "I found a really nice Martin for about $400."

"And I found a flute that's way better than what I have now. It's also about $400.

So I got a new flute. And Scott got a new guitar. Scott eventually paid Bob back, but I never did. I still feel a little guilty about it, but it was probably a minimal expense for them and we sure appreciated the patronage.

My Buddhist phase was over by now. I was embarrassed to chant where I could be seen or heard, and in any case I was getting impatient for concrete results. I looked back upon this as a failed experiment in spiritualism. However, I wish I had kept the beads.

Chapter 13: "Fuck Stockton!"

When you spoke to me
And you told me how you feel

—*When I Heard You Speak, Phil McKay*

We were so encouraged by the reception of "Ravel" at our UOP performance that we started thinking of a new project. Steve came up with an idea for "Fair Thunder." It was to be a story about a mythical giant who falls in love with a dewdrop. Winter comes and she disappears. Fair Thunder looks all Winter in vain for her. Mourning his loss, he gives up his search. In the Spring she reappears in his tears and he realizes that she never left him. The theme is the recurring cycle of time. It would be about 90 minutes long, featuring Bernie. Steve had a couple of good songs to start it off. The project never got beyond the concept stage.[*]

We continued playing at many small clubs around the Bay Area in 1973, saving our money and occasionally heading back south to Hollywood. It was getting to be routine but was occasionally broken up by concert gigs, such as when we played warm-up for Harvey Mandel in Sacramento at the Convention

---

[*] We performed two songs from Fair Thunder, "Fair Lady," and "Winds of Change" on a live KSAN broadcast from the Record Plant in Sausalito in October 1973.

Center, the site of my first gig with Stuart Little.

We played a lot of dinner houses in Sacramento, Tahoe, and the Bay Area as well as some Bay Area nightclubs, notably New Orleans House in Berkeley, Keystone West and the Condor (Carol Doda's club) in San Francisco, New George's in San Rafael, Inn of the Beginning in Cotati, and Sweetwater in Mill Valley. When we weren't playing we were spending a lot of time by the Blumenthal's pool or in the living room working on new songs. I really enjoyed the new flute and felt that my performance had gone up a notch.

Getting booked at the Great American Music Hall in San Francisco was a big break for us. Tom Bradshaw had refurbished and opened the Great American Music Hall in 1972 and it quickly became one of the top venues in San Francisco. We performed there with a number of world-famous musicians throughout 1973 and into 1974. The club was predominately jazz oriented, so our style fit very well. We shared the stage with Sarah Vaughn, Dizzy Gillespie, Stan Getz, Herbie Mann, Mongo Santamaria, Pharaoh Sanders, Al Jarreau, Buddy Rich, Carmen McRae, and many others. They weren't all jazz performers. We also performed with the Sons of Champlin, Asleep at the Wheel, Jerry Garcia, The Tubes, Bobby McFerrin, and others. Often on Tuesday nights we headlined and occasionally on a Friday or Saturday.

The gig with the Tubes was especially interesting. The GAMH is located next door to the famous strip club, Mitchell

Brothers Theatre. The U. S. Supreme Court had recently overturned an obscenity law that was intended to stop the distribution of the Mitchell Brothers movie, "Behind the Green Door." To celebrate their victory, the brothers had booked the GAMH for a private party. We played a long set and then left the stage while The Tubes set up. By this time the partygoers had taken full advantage of the open bar. Scott pointed out (I don't know how he always found this kind of stuff) that over in the corner near the stairs leading down to the basement dressing rooms there was a line of women in front of a guy taking pictures. As each one came to the front of the line, she pulled up her top for the photo. Some hiked up their skirts, too. The house lights seemed particularly dark that night, so I could only imagine what else was going on. None of us shared in the festivities because it was made clear to us before we started that this was a private party and we were just the hired help.

Another time we played two nights with Dizzy Gillespie, who had brought his wife to San Francisco. We spent a lot of time talking to them before the shows. They were very gracious and pleasant, some of the nicest people we had ever met in or out of the business. They gave us some "Dizzy Gillespie for President" buttons, which I lost ages ago. Conversely, Stan Getz (one of my early heroes) was not sociable at all. In fact, he even failed to show for his first set so we had to play two sets for the first show. Rumor had it that he was too drunk. After we were done with our set, the

101

house was cleared for the second seating. We played the warm-up set and then he came on with his backup guys. He was amazing. I'm glad I had a chance to see him perform.

Most of the others that we met were not actually mean but not real warm either. They simply did not pay too much attention to us. But there were a couple exceptions. Herbie Mann was arrogant and condescending to us low-class musicians. But Buddy Rich outdid them all in the obnoxious category. He had a reputation for being somewhat of an ass. He didn't disappoint us.

The GAMH dressing rooms were in the basement underneath the stage and dance floor. They weren't really rooms, but partitioned spaces with no ceilings, like cubicles in an office but with full height walls and doors exiting to a common area, which led to the stairs that emerged on stage right. As a consequence of this configuration, individual spaces were not soundproof. We usually occupied the same dressing room, furnished with a couch or two, a couple tables and several chairs.

Buddy Rich was scheduled for two shows that night, and we were the warm-up act for both shows. He was in the dressing room next door. It was about twenty minutes before the first show and we were getting ready to go on stage. Grode wasn't there that night, but Ron S., Bernie, and a few friends were with us, altogether about eight or ten people sitting there, talking and laughing, passing joints and drinking beer. Bernie was putting on his white face makeup while we started tuning up and jamming a little to warm up. We had barely started when all of a sudden the door burst open and Buddy Rich was standing there in his *gi* (he was a black belt in karate). His face was red and angry. He stood and glared at us for a few moments, then shouted, "You guys shut the fuck up. You're bothering me!"

"We're just trying to…" said Scott.

"And put out that fucking weed. What the hell's with you asshole hippies?"

He really hated hippies. His band had a strict dress code: Short haircuts, no facial hair, coats, ties and polished shoes. They all looked like Jehovah's Witnesses to me.

I tried to interject, "Hey, we're just getting ready to go up. We need to warm-up."

"Knock this shit off. I need it quiet. And I mean right now!" He stepped further into the room and intensified his glare. He was obviously accustomed to getting his way.

David K. stood up and started moving towards him. Buddy Rich clenched his fists and, even though it didn't seem possible, he became even angrier. Bernie saw the situation escalating so he stood and moved towards David K. Bernie also held a karate black belt as well as being well practiced in other martial arts. And, as I had mentioned before, he was probably the strongest person I had ever met. I was thinking to myself, "Bernie could beat the crap out of this guy. He's stronger, younger, and faster."

Everyone became very quiet. I don't know where David K. got the backbone to face Buddy Rich down. He usually tended to hang out more in the background. "Just wait a few minutes," David K. told him. "We'll be on stage really soon. We need to tune up." And then he stepped a little closer and stared him in the eye. Bernie went on full alert and moved just behind and to the side of David K.; poised, relaxed, and balanced on the balls of his feet. If Buddy Rich noticed Bernie's moves, he didn't acknowledge it. His attention was totally focused on David K.

Buddy Rich's temper was legendary. He was known for constantly terrorizing and belittling his band, which was made up of hand-picked top college jazz musicians from around the country. I don't know if anyone had ever tried to confront him, but he certainly did not take it well. "I'm warning you. I told you sons of bitches to knock it off," he threatened. "I want it fucking quiet and I want you assholes to shutup RIGHT NOW!"

"Come on, David…" Steve tried to get his attention. We were really worried about what might happen. The tension was building rapidly. David K. did not seem concerned.

David K. spoke up again. "Leave us alone. We're almost ready to go upstairs."

"Shut your fucking mouth or I'll shut it for you!" Buddy Rich yelled. His face was getting redder—blood pressure obviously rising.

We couldn't believe what was going on. Neither could Buddy Rich. The two of them glared at each other for a few moments. Then David K., taking a step closer and getting even more in his face, raised his voice and said very loudly and very slowly, "Don't...you...EVER...come to Stockton!"

"Fuck you! And fuck Stockton!" and with that he turned and stormed out. We finished tuning then went upstairs to the stage. We played a really good set and then watched his band. They totally kicked butt. The second show went off with no further incidents.

The GAMH became a regular place for us to play through 1973 and part of 1974. We had so many nights on the stage that Tom Bradshaw, the owner, had broached the possibility of us being put on retainer as house band. That idea became irrelevant when the band broke up in the spring of 1974.

In 1992 the club was sold to Claire and Kurt Brouwer, who ran it until putting up for sale in 1999. It is now owned and operated by Boz Scaggs, who also owns Slim's. The bookings have moved away from jazz towards more alternative, progressive and even retro. During the past few years I have seen performances by the Zombies, Love, and the Flamin' Groovies. [*]

Our next trip to L.A. was to meet with Eddie Choran. He had arranged for some studio time and wanted us to come down right away, so we planned another trip to Hollywood. Eddie said we could stay at his place, so we didn't need a gig to pay for a

---

[*] Coming full circle, in 2014 my daughter's band was the warm-up act for Flamin' Groovies.

motel. We loaded up the VW Microbus and worked out our transport. Steve didn't want to drive down because it took too long, so he bought an airline ticket. In 1973 a ticket to L.A. was only about $25-$30. Ron and David K. were riding in the VW, Scott was driving his pickup with his girlfriend. That left Bernie and me to find transportation.

The Blumenthals loaned us their Mazda station wagon for the trip. We all left Kentfield together. There was no room in the VW or Scott's pickup for Steve, so Bernie and I took Steve to the San Francisco Airport to catch his plane, then we headed for L.A. Bernie and I stayed reasonably close to the speed limit until we hit the turnoff for Highway 5 and then hit the gas. This Mazda was one of the early models with a rotary motor and it was really fast.

"What time does Steve's plane arrive in L.A.?" Bernie asked me.

"I think at 3:00 o'clock."

"Think we can beat him there?"

"Let's go!"

We cruised most of Highway 5 at 100-105 mph. Whenever we saw a cop we slowed to 85 mph, only 10 mph over the limit. One time a CHP was pacing us in the next lane for about 3-4 minutes. We weren't particularly worried because we weren't smoking or holding. We just looked at him and smiled, he smiled back and then he took off.

We arrived at Eddies about 2:30 and told him what we had

planned. Steve had made arrangements to call Eddie when he arrived so someone could pick him up at the airport. We waited for the phone to ring. Shortly after 3:00 o'clock it rang and I picked it up. "Hi, Steve," I said. A long silence followed.

"David?"

"Yea. You need a ride?"

"What are you doing there?" questioned Steve.

"Waiting for you."

"Oh geez…Well, I'm here. At the airport."

"We'll be there in about 30 minutes. Eddie and his girlfriend have dinner planned at his house."

Back at Eddie's we were all gathered in his living room. "You guys make yourselves at home. There's beer in the refrigerator. Carol (not sure if that was her name) and I are going to go get stuff for dinner. We'll be back in about an hour or so."

So we followed his advice, opened some beers and started wondering out loud what was planned for us. I had a brainstorm. "Let's short-sheet Eddies bed."

"What's that?" asked Scott.

Ron S. started laughing—he knew what it was.

"Huh?" asked Steve.

I explained. "You take the bed apart, then fold the top sheet so that it looks like both sheets, but it's really folded in the middle so you can only get in halfway. The only way to fix it is to take the bed completely apart and remake it." We all thought this was pretty funny, especially since Eddie was not a tall person. So we all trooped upstairs. "Look very carefully at the way it's made. We have to make it look exactly the same."

So we carefully pulled the, pillows, blankets, and bedspread off, then folded the top sheet up and tucked it in so from the outside, it looked like a bottom and top sheet. We replaced the blankets, bedspread and pillows and admired our handiwork. It looked perfect. We were sitting around the living room drinking beer when Eddie and Carol returned with the groceries. We could hardly wait until nighttime.

After dinner we all sat around drinking beer and playing a few tunes. Eddie told us he'd been talking to Robert Stigwood and that's why we were down there to make another demo tape. We were pretty jazzed up about that but we still wanted him and his girlfriend to go to bed. Finally, they headed upstairs. We waited, giggling to each other. Soon enough we heard him yelling down stairs, "Very funny guys. Very, very funny. Thanks a lot!" Carol was laughing really loud.

We were laughing, too. "What are you talking about?" we yelled up. Or tried to anyway. We were really practically falling out of the chairs.

Chapter 14: Holy Flying Saucers

Sittin' here waitin'... anticipatin',
The pot of gold that I'll have

—*The Price, Steve Solari*

"JOY!" I wrote to Debbie in early April 1973. "I just found out RSO Records wants to sign us! Not sure if we're signed, but Stigwood loved the tapes."

When I wrote this, Steve and I were getting ready to leave for whatever club we were playing that night. Eddie Choran had told us that it looked really good and we were elated. It looked like our time had finally come.

Later that month, we were down in Hollywood and the rumors were spreading fast about Stuart Little signing with RSO Records. We were invited to a press release party for J. Geils Band that was held at a strip club in Hollywood called the Classic Cat. I got a pair of perfumed panties with the band's name printed on the butt that I sent to Debbie. After leaving the party, we had to go for a sound check at another location where we were performing "Ravel" later that night.

Still nothing definitive from RSO, so we returned to the Central Valley where we played in a club with Sal Valentino.

The manager offered us $75 or as much as $100 if he did well that night. Not much money, but as usual we were flat broke after the L.A. trip and willing to take what we could get. The room was practically sold out, even the standing room, probably about 400 people who were charged $3.00 at the door. The jerk manager cried poor and only paid us $75 even though he made a lot at the door and the bar.

We had a lot more Bay Area gigs lined up. Bookings were scheduled at the Long Branch, New Orleans House, and One World Family Center in Berkeley, Boarding House, Great American Music Hall, and Keystone Korners (West) in San Francisco, and Sweetwater in Mill Valley.

I got a call from Steve, who had gone down to Los Angeles with Grode to meet with Joe Salyers,[*] who was the manager for Three Dog Night, Steppenwolf, and Black Oak Arkansas. He was very interested in "Ravel" and wanted to find a producer (money guy) to put it on at a Hollywood theater, either Century City or the Forum. He was seeking a $250,000 production budget and an additional $30,000 advance for us. Just to stay consistent with our run of luck, somebody ambushed Joe Salyers as he walked out of the elevator in his apartment building. He was shot in the arm, although not seriously wounded. However, by the

---

[*] When we first met him he ran a financial management firm. After leaving the hospital he sold his company and went into personal management. He later became the GM for the Lincoln Center and the LA Philharmonic at the Hollywood Bowl.

time he recovered he had diverted his attention elsewhere and was no longer interested in us.

Now we were getting more desperate and running out of money all the time. We looked into getting booked on an ocean liner so we could travel for free, get paid, have regular meals, and maybe find an audience in Europe. The biggest attraction to this idea for me was that we would be away from Stockton for a long time. It was a good idea, but not easily realized, so it fell by the wayside—just another pipe dream.

I was hanging out at the house I shared in Stockton when the doorbell rang. It was a couple of Jehovah's Witnesses with a 5-year old daughter in tow, all in their "Sunday Best." The two women told me stories about the Garden of Eden, the Fall, and a Paradise on Earth again. Then they tried to sell me a book called "Is the Bible Really the Word of God?"

I thumbed through it and said, "I have my doubts about that but I have a book that I want to give to you. I retrieved a book I had just read titled "Letters from the Earth," by Mark Twain and asked her to read the first 100 pages. She (the spokesperson) was shocked. Then I told her that the Buddhists also said a Paradise was coming, which led into a discussion of God's Law and wolves eating rutabagas and the lion lying with the lamb. Finally she got tired of playing verbal cat-and-mouse with me and launched into a pitch for Bible readings at home. Then she asked me, "Do you know how we print our books so cheaply?" (They were only 25 cents each.)

I looked at her and answered, "You have an 'in' with the publisher?" Her partner laughed and I kept a straight face. Finally they gave up on me. As they were leaving, I suggested once again that they read Mark Twain's book. I closed the door, sat down and laughed for about five minutes. They even left me a couple books and didn't charge me.

This was not the only spiritual connection I made outside of my short-lived Buddhist conversion. Our gig at the One World Family Center was a unique experience. They booked us, offering all of the door and a meal. We agreed to let them put another band on the bill, too. When we got there we discovered that this was a commune and they were all very skinny, spacey people. They only served a macro-biotic diet, so all we got for dinner was a bowl of brown rice. Looking around the room we observed that the walls were covered with huge murals of flying saucers, comets and other astral-themed subjects.

We set up and started to play. Debbie sat by the door collecting the $1.00 door charge. Commune members didn't have to pay. The place started filling up and then our "hosts" asked if they could put another band on. We said OK, so they brought out four or five commune members who called themselves The Spiritual Brotherhood. As soon as they began, to play the commune members paired up and started giving each other back massages. The band played some kind of mystical space music with a lot of droning and wordless tunes.

They finished playing and we came back. Then they wanted another band. They called themselves Brown Rice Mambo. It was pretty much the same guys as the first band with one or two additions, but the music was almost the same. The next band they put on stage was Brothers and Sisters In Harmony. You guessed it—the same as one of the previous bands except this time they had two women droning. It sounded almost the same. I don't know how many bands they put on stage but they were all different permutations of the same handful of musicians and all seemed to be playing the same song. What was really irksome was that the One World Family Center bands got more applause than we did.

We talked to various members and found out more about the commune. Their leader was Allen Michael, the Cosmic Messiah. He had a Direct Mind Link with the Inter-Galactic Space Command Complex. The commune members were patiently waiting in their storefront in Berkeley, where they were convinced that some day soon Jesus would land his Holy Flying Saucers in front on Telegraph Avenue and carry off all the members bodily to Heaven. We didn't see Jesus arrive while we were there, and apparently he still hasn't arrived because the OWFC has relocated to Santa Rosa, CA., Maybe they need more landing room for the Flying Saucers? [*]

It had been many months since Grode last performed with us so we were trying something new. We brought in a drummer to audition, but it didn't work out. So we had to split the door five ways. "Debbie," I asked, "how much did you take in?"

She looked in the basket. "Eight dollars."

"That's all?"

"Almost everybody that came in is a commune member."

We walked out with $1.60 each. Debbie later told me that she had put in $5.00 from her purse.

We were starving and all we'd had was a bowl of brown rice so we went to Denny's in Berkeley after the show. The place was infested with cockroaches and it seemed like all the street weirdos had decided it was time to make an appearance. It looked like the circus sideshow was getting off work at the same time we were.

By the end of summer 1973, most of us were living in a sublet house in Sausalito, which was a handy location for all our Bay Area gigs. We were playing three to four nights a week, sometimes more. I wanted to play six nights a week because I was

---

[*] This group has often been confused with another group centered around flying saucers, "Heavens Gate." On March 26, 1997, 39 members of the group committed mass suicide in order to reach what they believed was an alien spacecraft following Comet Hale–Bopp

114

finally seeing a little steady cash flow. Some months I made as much as $350.00. We had pretty much lost touch with Grode by this time, so we were very surprised when he showed up at the house one night with Eddie Choran. I was very unhappy to see Grode. Not understanding that he was schizophrenic, I was uncomfortable with his increasingly unpredictable behavior. There was a growing mutual animosity. I managed to avoid interacting with him while he was there. Eddie was still working with Robert Stigwood Organization and had not given up on us. He claimed he had some other deals pending, but I didn't believe him. There had been so many failures.

In August and September 1973 we were playing a lot around the Bay Area and we started getting reviews in the newspapers. Phil Elwood, the music critic for the San Francisco Examiner wrote a piece in August 1973 titled "A Little Known Astonishing Band." He referred to our regular Tuesday night headlining at the Great American Music Hall, commenting on our "…astonishingly competent original repertoire." He continues, "When all this goes on, and the group is singing, the dance floor fills and a feeling of a country down-home jamboree permeates the room."

Joel Selvin, writing for the San Francisco Chronicle noted "…smooth, satisfying vocals, intricate and musical instrumentals, mime by one Bernard Bang and a total, unified sound all its own.

Seated on stools on stage, the relaxed demeanor of the musicians reflected the restrained and delicate nature of their music."

"Long instrumental flights—led usually by guitarist David Kemp or flautist David Hoiem—provided the groundwork for the fanciful, lyrical songs. The individual sound takes on constantly changing shape during the performance…"

Maybe as a result of the recent press, we got booked at the new location of the Matrix in San Francisco. The Matrix was originally a tiny club on Fillmore Street in San Francisco, started by Marty Balin and his dad, primarily to give the Jefferson Airplane a place to play. It hosted several prominent bands, but closed in 1971. We never played there, but it was reopened in 1973 on Broadway in a bigger location, where it lasted only three months. We were scheduled to be the warm-up band for Sons of Champlin for two nights, October 19-20, 1973.

Much to my disappointment the Sons of Champlin had to cancel and a substitute band was found. The Wailers (before they were called Bob Marley and the Wailers) had been left at loose ends in Las Vegas after a gig was cancelled there, so the Matrix booked them for the headline act. The 700-seat club sold out both nights. We were very surprised when we came out on stage and discovered that the audience for The Wailers was 90% black. To our surprise we got a very warm reception and even played an encore.

After our set, I stopped by the Wailers dressing room to see what was happening. I had never heard Reggae before, and certainly didn't know who Bob Marley was but I knew about Rastafarians and ganja. The place was packed with bodies but I could barely see across the room because the smoke was so thick. A few people commented favorably on our set and then passed me the largest doobie I had ever seen. It was about eight inches long and three-quarter inch diameter and was putting out huge clouds of smoke. Somebody told me it was called a "spliff." I took a hit and passed it on and then another one came my way. The hits kept coming for some time until the Wailers went on stage and rocked the house. What a memorable introduction to Reggae!

KSAN-FM was the premier Bay Area radio station for contemporary music. They broke away from the Top 40 format in the late 1960's and pioneered playing full-length songs that were longer than three minutes. The radio station also featured regular broadcasts of live performances from the Record Plant recording studio in Sausalito. We were asked to perform for a one-hour broadcast segment on October 21, 1973. We came in the studio and set up. We were allowed to have a small audience, so we brought in a few friends, maybe eight or ten. We also had Bernie come so that it would feel more like a stage performance, although he declined to put on whiteface.

Steve and Scott set the tempo for each song but they were so nervous about playing for an unseen audience that they started each song much faster than usual. It was a good thing that we were very tight from our nightclub gigs four or five times a week. David K. and I had a bit of a hard time with our leads because they were so much faster than we were used to. At the time we thought the broadcast was a disaster because everything was so rushed, but listening to the recording today, we discovered that we were not as bad as we thought at the time.

Chapter 15: The Guy in the Yellow Ferrari

When the times are blurred from the past,
and life is but a wave goodbye,
I then recall a withering dream

—*Shining Through, Steve Solari*

Steve was weaving frantically through the traffic on Sunset Blvd. early one evening. The L.A. traffic was not heavy but he was racing the Green Hornet up to the stop lights, and then jumping ahead as soon as they changed.

"Steve, what are you doing?" asked Scott.

"I need to catch up with that guy."

"What guy?"

"Up ahead. In the yellow Ferrari. He just pulled out of Dark Horse Records. * I've got to catch him."

"What for?"

"He looks important."

The traffic gods were with us. Steve screeched to a stop right next to the Ferrari just as the light turned red. "Quick! Give me a tape!" He grabbed a cassette, jumped out of the car and ran over to the Ferrari and began tapping on the driver's window. The window rolled down and Steve handed him the cassette. "I think you'll like this," he said to the guy, who took it, looked at it and

---

* George Harrison's record label after the breakup of Apple Records.

119

then the light changed and he took off. Steve made it back in the car and we continued down the street.

"Who was that?" asked David K.

"Hell if I know," replied Steve, "but he's got our tape now." Little did we realize that this incident would evolve into the biggest missed opportunity of our career to date.

The next day, David K., Steve, and I were scheduled to practice with Richard Torrance and his drummer in preparation for doing some studio work for him. He was cutting an album for Leon Russell's new label, Shelter Records. We were getting paid Union scale, $30 an hour, for three hours of session time at Sound City Studios. The recording went well. The piece was seven minutes long but took six people 24 hours of studio time to get the final mix. The LP was released in early 1974. Our session was not included in the release.

We continued our stay in L.A. performing Ravel at a few colleges in the area.

Just when we had planned to leave L.A. Steve got a call from the guy in the yellow Ferrari. "Hi. This is Lou Adler and I like the tape you gave me. When can you come to the Whiskey A Go Go to meet with me? I'd like to hear you play."

"Any time that works for you."

"Can you come over tomorrow around 11:00 in the morning?"

"We'll be there."

We showed up about 10:30 and waited for him to appear. We introduced ourselves and thanked him for listening to us, then he ushered us into the dark club. "I'm sorry, I don't have a PA guy here."

"No problem," I replied. We'll just play right here." We pulled up some chairs in a circle on the floor in front of the dark stage then set up the bass and guitar amps. Scott was on acoustic and didn't need an amp, and of course the flute didn't need miking.

"This is really cool," said David K. He chuckled and said, "I love playing acoustic."

"You guys can really do this?" Lou asked.

"Oh yeah, said Scott. This is how we practice." Then we played a few tunes, all sitting together in a circle about eight feet across—very intimate.

"I'm impressed," Lou told us. "I'll see what I can do for you."

Returning to Northern California we wanted to get more bookings at Tahoe where we usually made pretty good money. We secured several nights at Yanks Station in Meyers, CA, which is just west of South Lake Tahoe. We were really counting on the income from this gig because we were flat broke from all our recent trips down south. We signed a contract for the week to guarantee the income—it was the one and only time we had ever signed a contract for a live performance.

A week before our booking at Yanks Station we got a call from Lou Adler. "I got a gig for you guys. Can you come down to the Whiskey next week? I have Seatrain booked and you would be the perfect warm-up band for them."

What a dilemma. We desperately needed the money from Yank's Station and couldn't afford another trip to L.A. On the other hand, this was Lou Adler and the Whiskey A Go Go… Several hours of intense discussion followed, with tempers flaring on all sides. Finally I said, "If we cancel this contract we may never work at Tahoe again. We can't get this reputation because this is our main income up here."

Steve called him back. "Mr. Adler, we really appreciate the opportunity, but unfortunately we are already contracted for a performance on that date and we can't break the contract. We'd be happy to come any other time."

"Well, that's too bad. It would have been an ideal booking for you. I'll keep you in mind but I don't have a spot for you in the future."

So we played our gig at Tahoe and later determined that we had probably made the biggest mistake of our lives. Who knows, it could have been another dead end or opened a lot of doors for us. We never had another chance to play at the Whiskey. Lou Adler was very influential at that time and is now one of the wealthiest people in the music business.

While we were playing at Yank's Station it was once again snowing very heavily. On Friday night after we were done I was sitting at the bar having a beer when an older lady (probably in her late 30's, but "older" to me) came and sat next to me and struck up a conversation. She seemed a little out of place there since the crowd was mostly in their 20's. We talked for a bit and then she told me, "I've got a really nice place out in the country near here and my husband is away for a couple more days. It's just me and my sixteen-year-old daughter there by ourselves. How would you like to come out with me?"

I considered the idea. It was intriguing.

"I can tell you, you'll have a really good time," she said.

I thought about it. I was worried because so many things had been going so wrong lately. In my mind's eye, I saw her husband coming home unexpectedly, then me jumping out a window naked into a three-foot snowdrift and having to figure out how to survive and make it back to civilization. "I really appreciate the offer, but I'm sorry I'll have to say no," I told her. She left, we put away our instruments and retired to the motel next door where I was sharing a room with Ron S.

I guess missed opportunities were in the air.

Ron and I entertained ourselves until early morning by imagining that the place was haunted with the spirits of the Indians that used to live there. It was weird because we felt a presence and even talked about it the next morning.

123

Chapter 16: Flameout

Here I stand on sinking sand
I must have lost my way

—*Sinking Sand, Phil McKay*

In January 1974, I finally had my own place to live. We were playing a lot around the Bay Area and I was getting a small but nearly predictable income, so I found a room to rent near San Francisco City College. I brought all my worldly possessions with me: a suitcase, my flute, and a milk crate of record albums. The proximity to the school allowed me to sneak into the practice rooms in the music department during the day.

Rose, a middle-aged Filipina, had a two-bedroom house painted blue inside and out. She rented out an in-law apartment in the basement to a WWII vet with a prosthetic leg and the two bedrooms in the back of the house were rented to college students. Rose slept on a couch in the living room. We had kitchen privileges and shared the bathroom. Rent was $75.00 a month.

Because I had a financial obligation, I began keeping a ledger to track my income and expenses. My first entry was January 29 where I noted a balance of $93.59—my total net worth. On January 29 I received a royalty check of $67.37 from SRO Productions for the Superstars of Rock television show. Total income for February was $186.75. March was better at $263.75 and in April I had no income because I left the band on April 17.

We appeared regularly at clubs like the Sweetwater in Mill Valley, Generosity and Wharf Rat in San Francisco, and of course almost weekly at the Great American Music Hall. But internally, the band's family relationship was breaking down, a consequence of frustration at the lack of success, financial pressure, and escalating personality conflicts. We were all tired of running headfirst into one brick wall after another and the frustration was straining our relationships.

The realization that things were really not working came when we met with Jerry Weintraub [*] in L.A. David K., Ron S., Steve, Scott, and I met with him in his office in a high-rise building on Rodeo Drive. For a heavy hitter in the music business, his office was not particularly large or ostentatious.

"Welcome gentlemen, come in and have a seat," as he extended his hand. We all shook and introduced ourselves. "I've heard a lot about you and I can offer you something of great interest."

"We'd love to hear what you have to say," said Ron.

"OK. Here's the deal. I'm putting together a tour with a very well known band. I'm not at liberty to say who at this time,

---

[*] He managed and produced John Denver. He also managed or promoted concerts for such musical acts as Elvis Presley, Led Zeppelin, The Carpenters, Frank Sinatra, Neil Diamond, and The Moody Blues.

but I need a warm-up act to go on tour and I think you're the right guys."

"When is this taking place?" asked Steve.

"The dates are not fixed, but probably starting in about 90 days."

"Well of course we're interested," I told him. "It sounds like a great opportunity."

"Good. I'll have a contract written up for you to review and sign."

"What else besides the tour would be in the contract?" asked Ron.

"Well, I'd like to produce your work and get placement with a record company, so it will have the usual stuff about royalties, publishing, and upfront costs"

"I don't care about that stuff," said David K. as he paced nervously around the office. "Just be sure that you put in there that I will get wood paneling for my Volkswagen van."

We kind of let this comment slide and went back to discussing contract terms. "We know how the revenue works and it is very important to us to keep artistic control and retain some of the royalties and publishing. We're looking for a 50/50 split," Ron stated.

Jerry looked at us, somewhat surprised. "Do you know what you're asking? You guys have no track record. You're not really in a position to ask for that."

"Just make sure I get wood paneling for my van," jumped in David K.

I interjected, "David, never mind that. If this works out you'll be able to buy any kind of paneling you want."

Now Jerry looked really surprised.

"I just really want to get paneling in my van," repeated David K. "It would be so cool."

"Why are we talking about lumber?" asked Jerry. "I've never had anyone ask for something like this before."

"David," from Steve and me almost in unison. "Don't worry about it. We'll buy you paneling."

The discussion moved to revenue and went downhill from there. Jerry was getting impatient, even angry with us. "I don't believe you guys. You're not serious. You don't understand how the business works. You're just wasting my time and yours. This meeting is going nowhere." Then he got up from behind his desk, walked to the office door and opened it. "Wood paneling…" he muttered to himself, shaking his head, as he held the door open.

We slowly shuffled out, totally dispirited. We knew we had blown it. We were disillusioned and knew that this time we could only blame ourselves for another failure.

We never heard from him again. As it turned out, the tour would have been with the Rolling Stones.

After this meeting we began a slow withdrawal from each other. Our rare practice sessions were very low key and lacked enthusiasm. I began to feel particularly ostracized. In the past, I presented lots of ideas for arrangements, inserting solo passages, trying different licks and harmonies, and we tried them out. Now, my ideas were mostly ignored. It was like breaking up with a girlfriend who no longer wanted me around. Once an integral member of the group I was now treated like an outsider. I could see where this was leading and I determined that it was very likely time to move on.

I had heard from somewhere that the band had been practicing without me and was auditioning a drummer without behind my back. My unhappiness and sense of alienation increased. On the other hand, I was tired of the repeated failures and of constantly being broke. I had to decide where my life was headed.

I sat down and wrote a letter to my bandmates, which I planned to give to them if it became necessary:

To the Stuart Little Band,

We have come a long way and put a lot of effort into trying to make a go of it in the music business. Unfortunately, we have only had failure after failure. I have now come to a crossroads in my life and I must make a decision about my future.

I have to get a job with a steady income. I want a home and medical insurance so that I can marry Debbie and raise a family. Playing in a band does not provide these for me. I need to quit playing music and devote my time and energy to building my future. It's been a great experience for me, but now it's over. Best wishes to all of you and good luck.

I came to our gig at the Great American Music Hall on April 17, 1974 with the letter folded up in my pocket. I wanted to force the issue because I was going nuts with the rejection I was feeling. I walked into the dressing room downstairs and everyone was there. "Hi guys. What's goin' on?"

"Oh nothing."

In the past, we had always worked together on a set list, so I asked, "You got the set list ready?"

"Yea, we already put it together."

" I have a very important question…"

"Yea?" asked Steve.

"Is it true that you have been practicing without me?"

"Well, yes," replied Scott.

"And is it also true that you have been auditioning a drummer without letting me know?"

"Yea, that's true," said Steve

"Does that mean that I am no longer a part of the band?"

"Well, not exactly," said Scott.

Then David K. glanced up from his guitar and chimed in. "I don't want him here. Either he goes or I go."

I looked around and said, "It's obvious what's happening." I didn't want to get fired, so I had to quit first. "I'll make this easy for you guys," and handed Steve my letter.

He read it to himself, then asked me, "Can I read this out loud for everyone?"

"Sure. It's for all of you."

He read it aloud and everyone was very quiet. "Do you really mean this?" Scott asked me.

"Yes. I know I'm not wanted here," I said. "I need to make some changes in my life."

As the guys picked up their instruments to go on stage, Steve asked me, "Are you coming?" My flute was still in its case under my arm.

"Why should I? I'm no longer a part of this band." David K. just glared at me as he walked by.

The three remaining members went up and played the last performance of the Stuart Little Band at the Great American Music Hall without me. I went upstairs and had a couple drinks at the bar, then went home. It would be a long time before we met again.

Chapter 17: Grode

I seek a ray of hope, while in the abyss I grope...
Something to heal my heart and soul

—*Desolation, Phil Mckay*

As time went on, we all drifted our separate ways. I took a day job at a drapery fabric wholesaler, measuring and cutting bolts of fabric. It was a union job with medical benefits, vacation, and holidays. Although it was really boring, for the first time in my life I was making more money than I was spending.

I still had long hair and a full beard, and was totally dedicated to being a musician. I had not had lessons since my college days almost five years earlier so I took private flute lessons at the San Francisco Conservatory of Music. I eventually earned the first flute chair in the second string orchestra. I was convinced that if I kept up my music, the big break would come some day. Bernie and I sometimes performed on the street near Fisherman's Wharf and Aquatic Park. I also played sax in a German oompah band that rehearsed at the Schonstein Organ Factory.

In June 1974 I asked Debbie to get married and she said yes. I bought a ring for $202 and we agreed that we did not want a big ceremony because we would have to pay for it. We had not set a date and I was still living at Rose's house.

We wanted a place of our own, so we kept saving. I was bringing home about $300 per week and she was working part-time at Woolworth's downtown on Market Street. By February 1975 we had enough saved to look for an apartment, about $1,000 each. We found a one bedroom with garage on the second floor of a 12 unit building in the outer Richmond District of San Francisco for $185 a month. We had no car, but got around on a small motorcycle and SF Muni. We bought a second-hand bed, got some hand-me-down tables and chairs and bought a sofa and loveseat set and moved in. I continued rolling fabric and Debbie stayed part-time at Woolworth's while attending San Francisco State University to get a teaching credential. We were very much in love and very happy. We married in August 1977 and lived in that apartment for almost six years.

In 1975 Scott was playing in the showroom orchestras at the South Lake Tahoe casinos. He needed a roommate to help with the rent, so Grode moved in with him. Grode had changed a lot in the past couple years, and not for the better. He was now very withdrawn and had extreme difficulty coping with the daily business of living. "There was a very hot chick at the unemployment office who was interested in him. They seemed to click and played tennis together," Scott told me. "There were other women interested, too. He was a chick magnet but couldn't deal with it." The long slide downhill into his private world began to dominate his life.

He steadily became worse. "He reminded me of Howard Hughes," related Scott. He would hide out in his room for days on end, never coming out to eat. When he did, he would not talk to anybody. His fingernails grew long and his hair was dirty and stringy. His clothes were wrinkled and smelly and his personal hygiene was sorely lacking. He didn't exactly hear voices, but he claimed he was receiving electromagnetic signals from the universe directly into his brain. Scott was busy trying to advance his career and had no idea how to deal with Grode's affliction. In 1975 little was known about schizophrenia.

After living together for a year and watching Grode's condition steadily deteriorate, Scott had to do something. "I called his parents and told them that he was in really bad shape and needed professional help. They agreed, so I talked him into getting on a bus and going to his parents' home in Marin County."

Grode's Mom called Scott to thank him for his help and informed him that Grode had been placed in a facility where he would receive the help he needed. Scott breathed a sigh of relief and found another roommate. He was glad to be able to focus on advancing his career.

A couple months later, Scott got a phone call from Jesse, the Mexican gardener at UOP. Grode had left (or escaped) from the facility and taken a taxi from the Bay Area to Stockton to see Jesse. Grode was convinced that Jesse was a shaman[*] and could

---

[*] see Chapter 5, p. 36.

provide him with a mystical understanding of the universe. Grode had no money, so Jesse had to pay the cab driver about $200 for the fare. "Can you come get him?" asked Jesse. "He's not making any sense."

"I'll come down," said Scott. He drove to Stockton, paid Jesse for the cab fare and returned to South Lake Tahoe with Grode. "It was most bizarre," said Scott. "He was even in worse shape than when I last saw him. He seemed sedated and said that he was being poisoned where he was being kept."

"I felt bad but I couldn't handle it and gave him an ultimatum. He had to go back to his parents. I put him on a bus back home. His mom kept calling me but I didn't want to deal with Grode so I ignored the phone calls."

Somehow in early 1976 Grode got his life back on track. He had a burst of energy and wanted to make another grab for the brass ring. I got a phone call one night. "Hi, David. It's Grode."

I was surprised to hear from him. "Hi Grode. What's up?"

"I want to get the band back together with Bernie, John Casserly, and the dancers to put on "Ravel.""

"Really? Have you talked to the other guys?" It had been a long time since I had any contact with them.

"Yea. They're all set to go. Steve will come back from Salt Lake for a few days, Scott and David want to do it. Bernie has agreed and I've talked to John Casserly about leading a dance company."

I was unaware of the turmoil he had gone through during the previous year. If I had known what had happened, I would have been even more surprised because now he was focused, energetic and brimming with enthusiasm. "Scott said we can write some string parts and get a small orchestra from UOP," he added.

"That sounds interesting," I replied. "Where would we do it?"

"I can get the Scottish Rite Temple auditorium in Stockton for a weekend."

"OK. I'm in."

I had been keeping up my flute practice and lessons, so I was confident I could do my part. I got together with Scott and we started working on the orchestration. Scott did most of the work with minor contributions from me. We wrote parts for four violins, three violas, and a cello. We also included a percussionist, Jonathon Meredith.[*] The conductor was Todd Barton,[**] and a drummer from UOP, Bob Stover.[***]

We staged a dance company featuring Bernie Bang, supported by John Casserly and five women dancers. Without Grode's initiative, planning, and hard work it would never have happened. He recruited the dance company, arranged for the venue

---

[*] His father is Burgess Meredith.

[**] After graduation from UOP he worked at the Oregon Shakespeare Festival in Ashland, Oregon full time where he became the Musical Director and Resident Composer. He retired in 2012, 43 years after his first performance in the Green Show in 1969.

[***] He is now the principal percussionist for the Stockton Symphony Orchestra.

and got all the band members back together. Posters, handbills and tickets were printed and articles placed in the Stockton Record newspaper. He kept us motivated and moving forward. The show was sold out for three performances, two evening and one matinee, with standing ovations at all shows.

Unfortunately, we garnered little attention outside of Stockton. The band made no money—all the ticket receipts went to pay expenses. It was the last hurrah of the Stuart Little Band. We came away with a very good live recording of the show but little else.

There were unintended repercussions from the show. I had played hooky from my day job to attend final rehearsals and the performance. When I tried to return to work with a forged doctor's note I got caught and was fired.

Worst of all, the failure was devastating to Grode, although at the time we didn't realize how hard he took it.

Afterword: Death...and Life

And listen if you will, the words of my last breath
My song is one of living, my song is one of death

—*The Letter, Gordon Clark*

Once again, the Stuart Little Band had made another leap into obscurity. The final performance of "Ravel" was an artistic success but beyond that...nothing. The lack of success was easily dismissed by all of us except for Grode. We were accustomed to failure by this time and held no big hopes for a Stuart Little revival, but Grode had huge expectations. The failure hit him particularly hard.

Some months after the performance we each received a contract from Gordon Clark, essentially divorcing himself and his contributions from the Stuart Little Band and our publishing company, Opporknockity Music. He stated exclusive rights to his poetry and music and partial rights to the songs that he had written jointly with some of us. We were surprised at this because none of this was ever in dispute. He wanted to have veto power for performances of "Ravel" and hold 50% rights to ballet stage productions. None of us signed the contract. We did not realize at the time that Grode's schizophrenia was worsening. We lost all contact with him after the middle of 1976.

"Gordy wanted to be a millionaire," said his sister, Susan. "He had this drive, this desire. He really wanted to go someplace and do something and be somebody."

Tragically, Grode eventually lost the battle with his demons. On December 27, 1978 he put a gun to his head and pulled the trigger. He was 30 years old.

Phil McKay, after his departure from Stuart Little Band, started another band called Merlin. Merlin became quite popular, playing many of the same Bay Area venues that Stuart Little did. He quit playing professionally in 1979, and in 1980 married his second wife Dori. In addition to a daughter, Lara, from his first marriage, he and Dori have a son, Jeffrey, and a daughter, Adrienne.

He became a senior partner in a winery in the Sierra foothills and then worked as a salesman for a wine company in Fresno, where he retired in 2009. On December 31, 2012 he died after a long bout with cancer.

Ron Schwartz worked as an installer and sales person for mobile electronics and traveled around California and even lived in Moscow, Russia for a spell. The day after his 40th birthday he suffered a heart attack and had an out-of-body experience while in the hospital. "I never lost consciousness and I had a conversation with God: If I get through this I'll throw down and become a teacher," he stated in an article published in the Stockton Record. He began work as a ski instructor at Mammoth Lakes while pursuing an online degree in Political Science at California State University Fresno.

Moving to Stockton to assist Bernie Bang with some home renovations, he began substitute teaching History at the local high schools. His passion for skiing soon motivated him to start the Edison High School Alpine Winter Sports Club, where there was immediate interest. Ron wanted to help underprivileged kids get exposed to skiing and snowboarding.

Bernie Bang continued performing after Stuart Little. In Paris, France, he began performing on national TV specials, MTV, and toured the world with the Emmy Award Winning Show, "An Evening With Diana Ross." Later, he moved around the country to help out friends. He was always generous with his time and expertise and helped many (including me) with home renovation projects. He lives in Stockton and still puts on the white face for street fairs, children's entertainment, and charity events.

David Kemp joined Phil McKay in Merlin in 1974 after the breakup of Stuart Little Band and played with them until that band split up. He separated from his family, severing all contact with his ex-wife, Mary, and his son, Damon. He continues playing around the San Francisco Bay area, mostly in Marin County. The last time I saw him several years ago he was divorced, out of touch with his family, and playing bass in a blues band at a street fair in San Rafael.

Stephen Solari married Patricia in 1974 after the breakup of the band. They moved to Salt Lake City so he could complete his doctoral studies in psychology at the University of Utah. Upon graduation in 1977 they moved back to the Central Valley and he began working for the California Youth Authority as a clinical Psychologist (California Department of Juvenile Justice). He retired from the CYA in 2013 after 35 years of service and lives in Stockton, Calif.

Even today he continues to write songs and perform solo in local coffee houses and clubs. He has compiled 5 albums of original material, some produced by Scott Liggett and James Lum.[*] Steve's albums are available on iTunes, CD Baby, and Amazon, under the name Solari and/or Stephen Solari. Patricia retired from teaching in 2014 and is pursuing her art. Steve and Pat have two grown children, Ian and Jessica, as well as three grandchildren.

Perry Karraker had his dream come true. Not the one about being a rock star, but he wanted to fly for the U.S. Air Force. After leaving the band he went to Officer Training School (OTS). Serving 29 years in the United States Air Force, he flew as a navigator and flight examiner. He had four different commands and retired with the rank of Colonel and was the U.S. Air Force Space Command's Chief of Space Training.

---

[*] James is a full time studio guitarist in Los Angeles as well as an independent music producer.

He then joined The Boeing Company as a Senior Manager in the area of International Flight Training Business Development. He has three grown sons, Steven, Regan, Preston, and a stepdaughter, Brie. Now retired, he lives in Colorado Springs, Colorado and enjoys exercise and golf. He still plays on the same drum set he had when he was in the band.

Because I had been fired from my day job after the "Ravel" performance, I picked up casual work through the ILWU Local 6 hiring hall and whatever other odd jobs I could find. In 1976 I was dispatched to Superior Coffee Company in San Francisco, where I worked my way up from sweeping floors to putting coffee in boxes and taping them shut, then progressed to other factory jobs. I eventually was promoted from the factory floor to a Route Sales driver, and then Account Executive, and finally West Coast Regional Manager for the renamed company, Sara Lee Coffee Company.

Debra and I married in 1977 and in 1980 gave birth to our daughter, Rachel. I still wanted to play music, so in 1983 I joined Undercover S.K.A., a ska band formed by my brother-in-law and his friends, where I played mostly sax. I played with this band until I had to give it up in 1990 because family obligations didn't mesh well with playing in Irish bars once or twice a week.

Retirement from Sara Lee in 2007 didn't even last one month. I accepted an offer from Peerless Coffee Company, a family owned roaster and distributor in Oakland, California. I left there in 2013 after 34 years in the coffee business and now spend time as a volunteer fitness instructor and gym rat at the local YMCA. During the winter, I'm a part-time ski bum. Debra retired from 30 years teaching elementary school in 2014. She is now pursuing her hobbies, including jewelry design and other creative endeavors.

Perry wasn't the only one of us who managed to live the dream. Scott Liggett has made a very successful career in the music business as a producer, composer, musician, and executive. After leaving the band, Scott was a staff musician for the house orchestras at Sahara Tahoe and Harrah's Lake Tahoe where he performed with many headline musicians including The Drifters and Frank Sinatra.

He then moved to Los Angeles where he co-founded the Alan Ett Music Group and Media City Sound in Hollywood. He wrote and produced sixteen Priceline.com music spots with William Shatner, produced music for NFL Super Bowl spots and composed music for the headline show at the Samuel Ochin Planetarium at the Griffith Observatory. His music has been heard in over 2,000 TV shows, commercials and promos. He currently has formed a digital graphic novel company, LNL Partners. Their first project is an animated graphic novel version of William Shatner's science fiction novel, MAN O' WAR.

Scott is a founding member of the International Documentary Association and a member of the Academy of Television Arts & Sciences, SAG/AFTRA, Society of Composers

& Lyricists and Ambassador for the Brubeck Institute at the University of the Pacific.

I believe I speak for everybody who was a part of the Stuart Little Band when I say that ultimately what was most important to us was the journey, not the destination. What we all shared besides the belief that our dreams could come true was the realization that if we had not chased the rainbow, we would have spent the rest of our lives wishing that we had made the attempt.

In Memoriam

Gordon "Grode" Clark
1948-1978

Burn the Wind

Burn the wheel, burn the wooden spoke

Burn the wind, I can't stand no more

Got to find my way 'round again

Got to live, got to feel the rain

Let me walk, where the waters run wild

Let me feel the mud between my toes

Don't ask me why, it's hard to say

May be love, may be just my way

Heal my weary soul, hold my hand

Burn the wisdom, I'm just a simple man

Treat me no more than a saplin' tree

I ask no more, just wanna be free

—Gordon Clark

Thanks

I want to thank Stephen Solari and Scott Liggett for suggesting this work and encouraging me to keep going. Also, for remembering things that I forgot and helping with the timeline. We had lots of laughs while recounting past events, many of which did not make their way into this story. I can't forget Perry Karraker, who provided insight into the early days of the Stuart Little Band as well as being a sounding board for my frequent rough drafts.

Grode's sister's donation to the "Gordon Clark Collection of the Stuart Little Band" at the UOP Library led to Michael Fitzgerald publishing a column in the Stockton Record about the band and Grode's suicide. For this, he deserves my appreciation for planting the seed that eventually became this book.

But most of all, I want to thank my wife, Debra, for her support and encouragement and the time spent proofreading each chapter, often several times. She also helped select the tracks included in the CD accompanying this book.

Of equal, if not more importance, is the foresight she displayed when she saved our correspondence from the time we met until beyond the demise of the band. These letters, bundled and tied in a red ribbon, were the most valuable source of information I could have wished for.

Peace be with you when you're young
You'll find contentment in the sun

Peace be with you when you're old
You'll find shelter in your soul

—*Peace Be With You, Stephen Solari*

Final song in "Ravel"

Track List: "A Mouse That Almost Roared"

#	Title	Time	Composer	Year
1	Better Man/Times of My Life	7:03	Phil McKay/ Stephen Solari	1969
2	Lord's Prayer	3:34	arr. David Kemp	1969
3	Smile at Me	5:45	Phil McKay	1969
4	Overture *	2:37	Gordon Clark David Hoiem Stephen Solari	1970
5	Burn the Wind *	4:47	Gordon Clark	1971
6	And When You Cry	2:05	Scott Liggett Stephen Solari	1971
7	Western Pacific	3:02	David Kemp	1972
8	Salt Lake to Stockton	3:28	Stephen Solari	1972
9	Smile	2:09	Stephen Solari	1973
10	Winds of Change **	2:56	David Hoiem David Kemp Scott Liggett Stephen Solari	1973
11	Know Yourself *	2:00	Stephen Solari	1973
12	Sunset Sunrise	6:47	David Kemp	1973
13	Spectrum Seekers	2:59	Scott Liggett	1974
14	The Pauper/The Letter *	3:55	Gordon Clark	1976
15	The Legend/Poverty Song *	4:57	Gordon Clark/ Stephen Solari	1976
16	Shining Through *	3:00	Stephen Solari	1976
17	Greyhound Bus/Arrival Song *	10:19	David Kemp/ Stephen Solari	1976

* from "Ravel"
** from "Fair Thunder"

Credits

Phil McKay: rhythm guitar & lead vocal: Better Man/Times of My Life, Smile at Me

Perry Karraker: drums: Better Man/Times of My Life, Smile at Me, Lord's Prayer

Stephen Solari: bass: (all songs) and lead vocal: Salt Lake to Stockton

Scott Liggett: rhythm guitar: (all songs except Better Man/Times of My Life, Lord's Prayer, Smile at Me), lead vocals: Smile, Spectrum Seekers, Shining Through, And When You Cry

David Kemp: lead guitar: (all songs), lead vocal: Burn the Wind, Western Pacific, Know Yourself, Sunset Sunrise, Poverty Song, Greyhound Bus/Arrival Song, Flute: Know Yourself

Gordon "Grode" Clark: all harmonica, lead vocal: The Pauper/The Letter, The Legend

David Hoiem: tenor sax, flute, and percussion

All personnel: backup vocals

Guest Appearances:
David LaFlamme: violin on Salt Lake to Stockton
Hilton Valentine: bongos on Sunset Sunrise

David Hoiem settled in San Francisco in 1974, just before the Stuart Little Band broke up. He makes his home there with his wife, Debra, and Gertrude, a 30-year old box turtle.

Now retired after 34 years in the coffee business, he enjoys gardening, reading, and working out at the local YMCA where he is a volunteer fitness instructor. His passion, which he shares with their daughter, Rachel, is Alpine skiing, which is why he spends so much time at the gym trying to stay in shape.

stuartlittleband@gmail.com